THE QUALITY ENGINEER STATISTICS HANDBOOK

The Quality Engineer Statistics Handbook©

Copyright© by German Candia, Memphis, Tennessee.

All rights reserved. No part of this publication may be reproduced, stored in a retrieval system or transmitted in any form or by any means, electronic, mechanical, photocopying, recording, scanning or otherwise, except as permitted by written authorization of the author.

NOTE: This publication contains the opinion and ideas of the author. It is intended to provide helpful and informative material on the subject matter covered. It is sold with the understanding that the author and publisher is not engaged in rendering professional services in the book. If the reader needs personal assistance or advice, a competent professional should be consulted. The author and publisher specifically disclaim any responsibility for any liability. Loss, or risk, personal or otherwise, which is incurred as a consequence, directly or indirectly, of the use and application of any of the contents of this book.

> LIMIT OF LIABILITY/DISCLAIMER OR WARRANTY: The publisher and the author make no representations or warranties with respect to the accuracy or completeness of the contents of this work and specifically disclaim all warranties, including without limitation warranties of fitness for a particular purpose. No warranty may be created or extended by sales or promotional materials. The advice and strategies contained in this book may not be suitable for every situation. This book is sold with the understanding that the publisher is not engaged in rendering legal, accounting, or other professional services. If professional assistance is required, the services of a competent professional person should be sought. Neither the publisher nor the author shall be liable for damages arising here from. The fact that an organization website is referred to this work as a citation and/or potential source of further information does not mean that the author or the publisher endorses the information the organization or website may provide or recommendations it may make. Readers should be aware that the internet site listed in this book may have changed or disappear between when this work was written and when it is read.

Portions of Information contained in this publication/book are printed with permission of Minitab, LLC. All such materials remain the exclusive property and copyright of Minitab, LLC. All rights reserved.

MINITAB® and all other trademarks and logos for the Company's and services are the exclusive property of Minitab, LLC. All other marks referenced remain the property of the respective owners. See minitab.com for more information.

To my wife Lyz, and to my son and daughter German and Karen

I hope your interest on science and the eternal pursue of the truth never fades away

"Untested and unsupported, is insufficient guarantee of truth"

Bertrand Russell

Table of Contents

1. Basic Quality Statistics 6

2. The Normal Distribution and Probability, Distribution Identification, Central Limit Theorem, and Other Useful Probabilistic Distributions............ 11

3. Statistical Process Control.. 18

4. Process Capability for Variable and Attribute Data.. 25

5. Measurement System Analysis for Variable and Attribute Data...................... 33

6. Confidence Intervals and Tolerance Intervals... 46

7. Hypothesis Test and Comparison of Samples.. 54

8. Sample Size Determination.. 67

9. Regression Analysis.. 74

References.. 84

Preface

After 15 years in factory floors working as a Supervisor, Superintendent, Manufacturing Engineer, Quality Engineer, Continuous Improvement Manager, and 12 years as a Design Quality Engineer, I had to learn about quality statistics from different books, from others, from experience, and obviously from my own mistakes. This was also a time before internet and electronic books.

Although the statistics and basic quality control topics that I learned in college were pretty good, I struggled applying them to everyday factory problems; that takes experience. Experience takes time, and that's something that we don't have in the industry.

I had to read from different books and manuals and take all kinds of advice in order to learn. Fortunately, I had a chance to take the Six Sigma training twice throughout my career. That was an eye opener. Everything started to make sense in a broader sense, the inference resulting from statistical analysis was the result of applying the scientific method, then the concepts and all the mathematics learned in college converged in a single time to create results, because statistical analysis without conclusions and results is almost useless.

In 2003, after my first Six Sigma training, I hit statistics as hard as my time allowed it; I was a Manufacturing Engineer and I got my assignments from one of the best Managers I ever had – Terry McGahuey - in a factory in Iowa. I applied the tools that I learned, and they provided results. If I had questions, my Master Black Belt was there to help me –Ken Bott, probably the best Six Sigma teacher that I have seen in the industry so far –. The problems we faced in that factory were not simple and the use of statistical tools and a scientific method was the only way to fix them or minimize them at least. Those methods moved us forward. Fixing one of these problems granted me the "Six Sigma Excellence Award for United States and Latin America" in 2004, for "Best Defect Elimination in Manufacturing" sponsored by Minitab® and organized by IQPC (Institute of Quality and Productivity Center, London, UK).

After all these years, and now coaching young engineers, still the question remained: why can't I find a single book that tells me most of the things I need in the day by day operations of a factory or design quality engineering? Furthermore, why didn't I learn the practical application of all these tools in college? Hopefully this book provides the answers to all the engineers that need to fix a problem or find answers in the industry and don't have a lot of time to read several books.

I highly encourage anyone who wants to learn more about quality statistics to take the steps necessary to build a strong mathematical background in statistics before moving to quality statistics, in case there is not a strong foundation. This will help you discriminate the good advice from the phonies and shenanigans in the industry – they are everywhere.

The theoretical background will help you see beyond the formulas and instructions. I don't touch mathematical theory or development in this textbook, as I said before, this is a handbook to help solve the problems that the Quality Engineer will find in the day by day operations and will help the student of quality control to solve the most common problems in quality statistics. I also wrote this handbook thinking that the Manufacturing, Process, and Quality Engineers would want to keep it on their desks to help them on the daily operations without having to develop formulas or find statistical tables.

Acknowledgements

I was lucky to have a good mathematical background from college and a great professor of statistics – Dirk Valckx – from the Universidad de las Americas, Puebla, Mexico. I may also add to my list of great college professors: Andres Ramos, Dolores Luna, Bulant Kozanoglu, as well as professor Scott Roberts from the University of Texas.

I can only dream of knowing as much as them.

A final recognition to my parents Manuel and Catalina Candia for pushing me and planting my first personal goals in my head.

Basic Quality Statistics

Descriptive statistics consist of numerical and graphical methods for describing data. To that end, we need to understand two simple definitions: a statistic is a value from a sample taken from a population, a parameter is a value taken directly from the population. Therefore, the statistic mean will be defined as "$\bar{x}$", and the standard deviation as "s", and the equivalent parameters will be "μ" and "σ" (population).

The choice between graphical or numerical methods depends on what type of data is collected. Although we are not going to focus on explaining or teaching the basic concepts of statistics i.e. how to calculate the mean, range, standard deviation, etc. We need to start by explaining the basic tools that can help us identify the shape of distributions, frequencies of events, detect unusual values or outliers, and concentration of data. Basic statistics can give us clues to select appropriate tools for subsequent engineering analysis.

In this chapter we will present graphical and numerical methods for variable and attribute data

There are two types of data: variable data and attribute data.

Variable data: occurs when a measurement has been taken on a **quantitative** characteristic, such as length, volume, thickness, etc. The methods to describe this type of data may include: sample mean, standard deviation, variance, median, maximum, minimum, and range.

Attribute data: occurs when classifying outcomes into a **qualitative** (non-numerical) characteristic, such as color, flavor, marital status, car brands, etc. Attribute data are sometimes called categorical data. The methods to describe this type of data may include: Pareto chart, bar charts, and pie charts.

Measurements of Variable Data

We can start by defining the numerical methods for measuring central tendency and dispersion (variability or spread).

Central tendency: The central tendency values are the mean, the median, and the mode.

- The **mean** of a set of measurements equals the sum of the measurements divided by the number of measurements.
- The **mode** is just the most frequent value of the sample
- The **median** of a set of data is the middle value when the data is arranged in increasing order.

If the sample mean is close or equal to the sample median, then the sampled data is distributed symmetrically. If the sample mean is well above the sample median, then the distribution of the data is said to be **skewed to the right**. If the sample mean is well below the sample median, then the distribution of the data is said to be **skewed to the left**. If the data is highly skewed, then the median is a better measure of central tendency than the mean.

Variability or Dispersion: The measure of variability encompasses the standard deviation, the variance, and the range, and measures the "spread" (dispersion) of the data. The standard deviation is an estimate of the dispersion between each data point and the mean.

- If all the observations are near the mean, then there is little variability in the data and the sample variance and standard deviation will be small. If, on the other hand, many observations are far from the mean, then there is a lot of variability in the data and the sample variance will be large.
- The formula for the sample standard deviation, where "n" is the amount of units in the sample, n-1 is called degrees of freedom:

$$s = \sqrt{\frac{\sum(x - \bar{x})^2}{n - 1}} \qquad\qquad s^2 = \frac{1}{N - 1}\sum_{i=1}^{N}(x_i - \bar{x})^2$$

Therefore, the variance is defined as:

- The sample range (sometimes denoted as "R") is not a very good measure of variability because it is based only on two data values, the minimum and the maximum. It is much more sensitive to "outliers" (i.e., extreme values) in data and can sometimes be a misleading indicator of the variability. Also, the range generally increases with sample size, unlike the standard deviation.

Now let's describe the analytical methods for attribute and variable data.

Pareto Chart

A bar chart is called a Pareto diagram (chart) when the bars are arranged in the descending order of height from left to right. The bars can represent frequency or relative frequency (i.e., each frequency as a percentage of total count in the sample) of each category.

Example

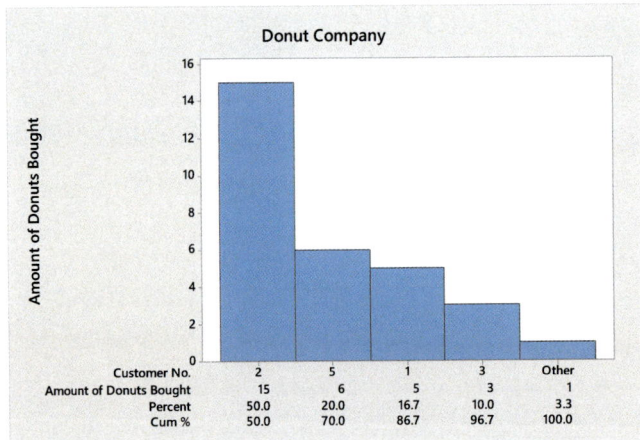

Histogram

A histogram provides a quick visual summary of the shape, spread, and location (concentration) of the distribution of data.

Following the same data from the "Donut Company" in the previous pareto chart, a histogram can be constructed as follows:

Example:

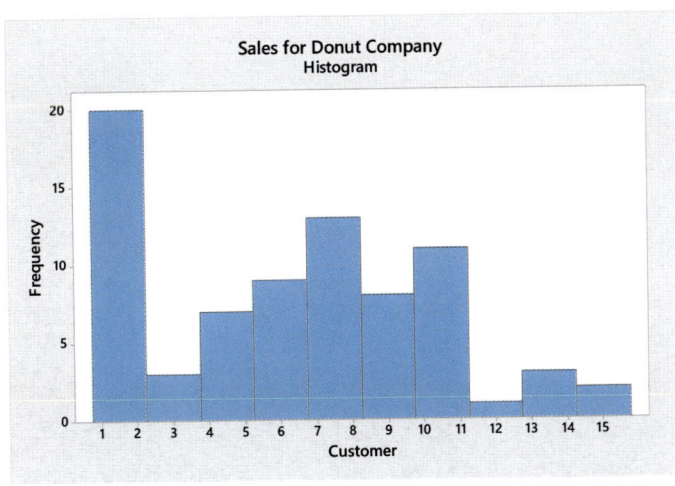

One needs to be careful not to choose too many or too few classes, class width is the X axis, while class frequency is the Y axis. Too few classes will disguise the actual spread of the data and too many classes exaggerate the spread. A piece of advice: first come up with an initial number of classes and then adjust that number based on the resulting histogram.

There are various recommended rules for determining the initial number of intervals/classes, k, for a sample containing measurements: n

1. Sturges' rule: k (group data) is approximately equal to $1+\ln n$.

2. 2^k rule: k is the smallest integer such that $2^k \geq n$

3. $\sqrt{n}$ rule: k is approximately equal to $\sqrt{n}$.

I recommend Rule 3 for obtaining the initial number of classes because it is easy to use.

One should always check the histogram to determine normality. In this case the histogram suggests a tall spike in the left tail, perhaps indicating non-normality. In the next chapter you will be provided with a way to perform a test of normality.

Box-Whisker Plots

- The **box-whisker plot (mostly called "boxplot")** is an exploratory data analysis tool that can be used to check for symmetry, visualize the data range, visually compare groups of data, and check distributional assumptions.

- Boxplots are very practical tools for **comparing two or more samples**.

- The **box** in the box-whisker plot extends from the **25th percentile** (1st quartile) to the **75th percentile** (3rd quartile).

- The **median** (i.e., the 50th percentile) is shown as a horizontal line in the box. If the median value does not fall at the mid-point of the box, it indicates lack of symmetry.

Box-Whisker plots are useful to visually compare the outcomes of multiple runs.

The **whiskers** of the box plot extend up to the minimum and down to the maximum data values.

For **normally distributed** data, the median is approximately in the center of the box and the whiskers are nearly of equal length – but do not jump into the assumption of normality yet.

Example

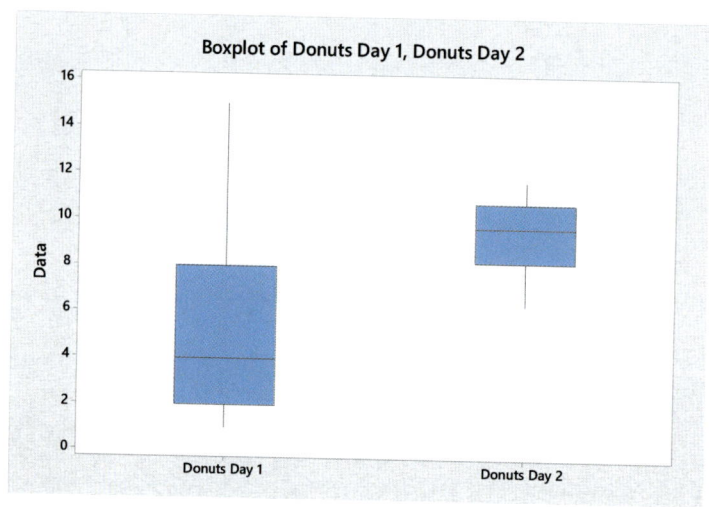

In this example, the Box-and-Whisker Plots show the comparison of donut sales day 1 and day 2.

- The variation in day 1 is larger than that of day 2 sales. This may be due to outliers and should be investigated.

- The plot for day 2 shows a slightly higher mean and median values compared to day 1 sales.

- Formal statistical tests can be carried out to test for statistical difference between the two groups using the methods which will be shown in the Hypothesis Testing section.

Variable Data – Descriptive Statistics

MINITAB has a very fast and practical tool to display descriptive statistics, a histogram, and a boxplot at the same time. Once you populate a column in the spreadsheet with the data, follow: Stat>Basic Statistics>Graphical Summary. You will get something like this:

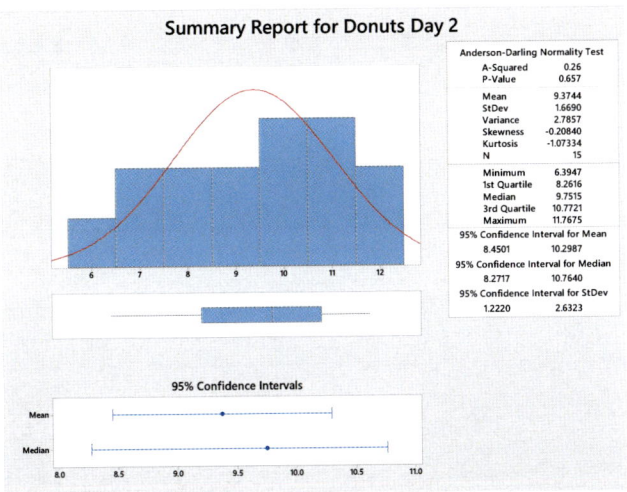

Note: Do not change the 95% confidence interval, we will explain more about it in the Confidence Intervals chapter of this book.

Variables Data - Skewness and Kurtosis

On the last chart you can see values for skewness and kurtosis. Skewness and kurtosis are measures of departure from normality. When measuring skewness and kurtosis of a normal distribution, the values are zero.

- A positive value of skewness indicates a long right tail compared to that of a normal distribution. A negative value indicates a long left tail.
- A positive value for kurtosis indicates that the distribution has big tails
- A negative value of kurtosis corresponds to distributions with a flatter top than the normal distribution.
- Skewness and kurtosis should not be used to demonstrate normality. They should only be used to explain an already demonstrated departure from normality.

Scatterplot

A scatterplot will help us visualize the process behavior for variable data, we can visualize and look for clusters, linear or not-linear behavior. In MINITAB we can do it through: Graph>Scatterplot

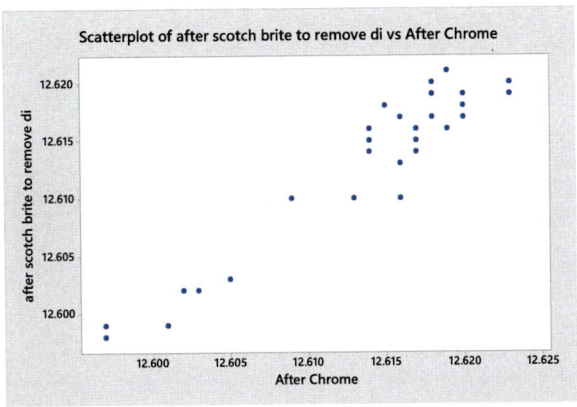

The Normal Distribution and Probability

The normal distribution is the basic model for statistical analysis, Karl Gauss and De Moivre before him, developed the current normal distribution model.

But before we move to the theory, let's see the normal distribution in simpler manner. We start by thinking that we are going to measure the height of the men in our city (in inches), we can start by measuring the first 10 men and we get this histogram:

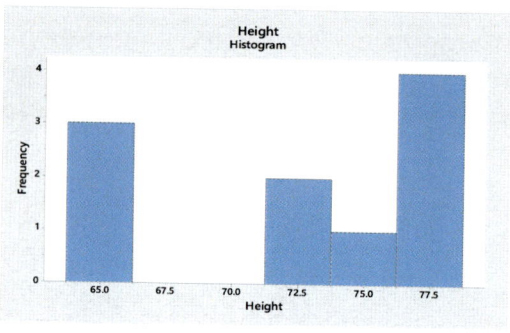

Now, if we keep measuring random men around us, and we have now 100, our histogram will look like this:

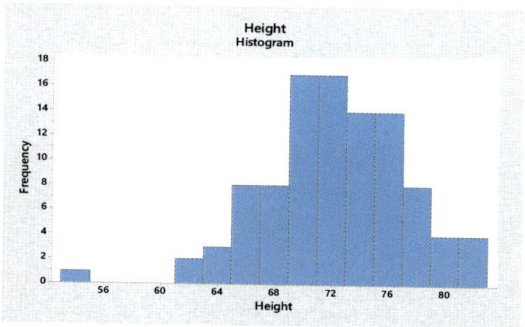

If we keep measuring, and then we collect 1,000 and eventually 10,000 measurements, our histograms will look like this:

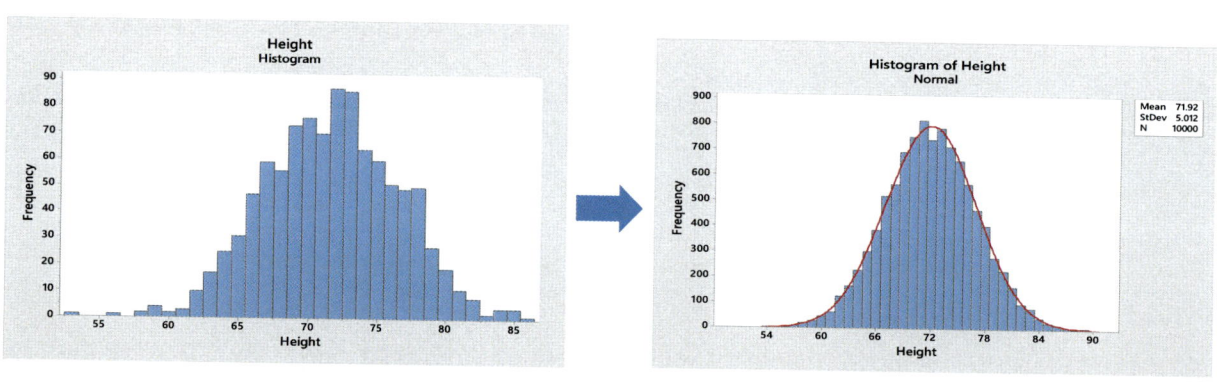

Therefore, thanks to calculous we can model the entire height population approaching the normal distribution model, which follows this equation:

$$f(x) = \frac{1}{\sigma\sqrt{2\pi}} e^{-\frac{1}{2}\left(\frac{x-\mu}{\sigma}\right)^2}$$

where σ is the standard deviation and μ the mean

This equation defines the normal distribution, where the limits of x are: $-\infty < x < \infty$

Therefore, cumulative probability density for the normal distribution can be calculated by this function:

$$\int_{-\infty}^{\infty} \frac{1}{\sqrt{2\pi}\sigma} e^{-\frac{1}{2}\left(\frac{x-\mu}{\sigma}\right)^2} dx$$

Where

$$\int_{-\infty}^{\infty} \frac{1}{\sqrt{2\pi}\sigma} e^{-\frac{1}{2}\left(\frac{x-\mu}{\sigma}\right)^2} dx = 1.$$

It means that the total probability under the curve is equal to 1, or 100% - in percentage of probability.

If we replace:

$$z = \frac{X - \mu}{\sigma}$$

We can perform a probability evaluation directly with Z. This is usually called: Standardization. It converts the random variable into a (0,1) random variable.

This mathematical model allows us to estimate probability of occurrence. In the past we had to use tables to calculate the values of the density under the curve (by following the equation mentioned before), now, any statistical software provides that for us.

One of the properties of the normal distribution is that it is symmetrical, therefore, the same distance from the mean "μ" to the right or to the left, provides the same value under the curve. If we calculate the values under the curve at a distance of: 1, 2 or 3 standard deviations (σ) from the mean (μ). We will have the following results:

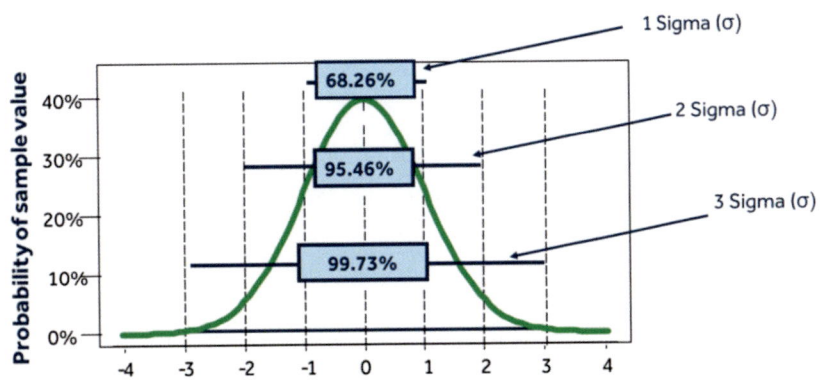

Number of standard deviations from the mean

Remember that the area under the curve is the cumulative probability, therefore, you need two points to get this value.

Note: While doing statistical analysis, if we immediately assume that our data is normally distributed, and it is not, we will get erroneous results. The values mentioned above – the sigma distance from the mean - will be invalid. Therefore, we must always check if our data is normally distributed.

Remember, there are three basic characteristics of the normal distribution:

1. It is symmetrical, 50% of the data on either side from the mean
2. The curve never touches the X axis
3. The total value of the area under the curve equals 1, or 100% ($-\infty, +\infty$)

Distribution Identification - Normality Test

There is more than one method to check for normality, they are named after their author(s): Anderson-Darling, Kolmogorov-Smirnov, Ryan-Joiner, Shapiro-Wilk. At the end, these tests are a way to assess how close our data is to the theoretical model of the normal distribution. In the industry, the test for normality most commonly used is the Anderson-Darling, which I prefer. In my experience, the Kolmogorov-Smirnov is more lenient.

Statistical software can do this test for us, the Anderson-Darling test will look like this:

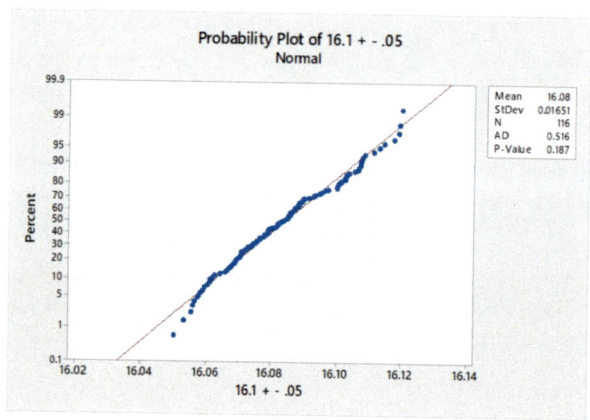

Since the "p" value is above of 0.05, we can determine that our data approaches the normal distribution, therefore we can treat it like that. For an explanation of the "p" value, check the hypothesis test chapter of this handbook (page 54).

Some books recommend the Shapiro-Wilks test as a better way to evaluate normality in small sample sizes, but in general, no tool is fully reliable with a small sample size.

Other Distributions

Other probability distributions will provide a different value under the curve because they are defined by different equations. Some commercial statistical software may have up to 16 different distributions identified. But we must always identify the process's behavior before we jump into a conclusion of normality or non-normality and make an inference based on that.

For example, I made a statistical analysis on heat exchangers. Specifically, this study aimed to find the aluminum shims distribution after the assembly process – before the brazing step. Since the final step on this process was performed vertically by a machine, the weight of the shims always fell on the bottom side of the heat exchanger. The number of aluminum shims per inch was bigger on one side than the other and the distribution looked like this:

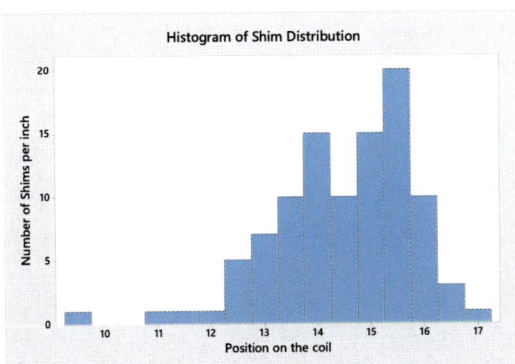

The root cause for this process behavior was gravity acting towards one side of the heat exchanger – it was a vertical process and the weight of the shims on one side was increasing the number of shims per inch on the other side. I identified that this process behavior was following the "Smallest Extreme Value" distribution (not the normal distribution), hence the curve looked like this:

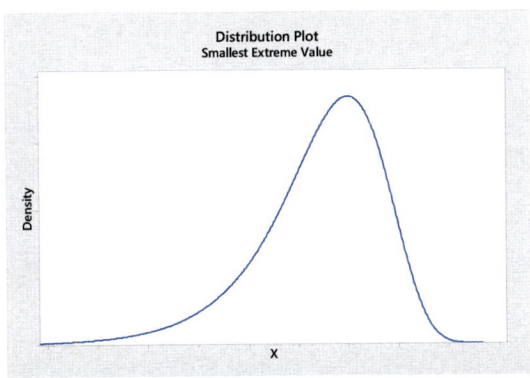

Therefore, making an inference for this process must follow the actual process behavior, not assuming normality.

Using MINITAB, we can identify the distribution of our process the following way: Stat>Quality Tools>Individual Distribution identification.

The Central Limit Theorem

This theorem states that the collective means of random samples drawn from any distribution will have an approximately normal distribution. Here the key word is: "mean". In other words, the distribution of the means tends to be normally distributed.

Based on our previous example, the individual samples per machine will always be non-normal (this is just the nature of the process), but we had 10 machines, so the averages from the samples from each machine will tend to be normally distributed.

T-Distribution

The T-Distribution is directly related to the normal distribution. This distribution is very useful for comparing a mean to a reference, or the difference between two means. The T-distribution looks like a normal distribution and it is also symmetrical, but the tails on both sides of the curve are wider, therefore, the probability at the tails is bigger than the normal distribution. This distribution can help us calculate confidence intervals and hypothesis tests – more about this in the hypothesis test chapter (page 54).

Notice the difference from the normal distribution in the following formula, degrees of freedom are n-1:

$$t = \frac{\bar{x} - \mu}{s/\sqrt{n}}$$

F-Distribution

This distribution is used to make inferences on two variances of normal distributions.

More about how to use this distribution in the hypothesis test chapter.

$$F = S_1^2 / S_2^2 \text{ with } n_1\text{-}1, n_2\text{-}1 \text{ degrees of freedom.}$$

χ^2 (Chi-Square)-Distribution

This distribution can be used for goodness of fit tests, sample variance from a normal distribution, and mostly to compare equality of two or more proportions. More about how to use this distribution in the hypothesis test chapter

$$\chi^2 = \sum_{i=1}^{n} \frac{(O_i - E_i)^2}{E_i}$$

Where Oi is the number of observations, and Ei the expected or theoretical frequency.

Weibull Distribution

The Weibull distribution is mostly used in reliability analysis (time to failure).

$$f(x; \lambda, k) = \begin{cases} \frac{k}{\lambda}\left(\frac{x}{\lambda}\right)^{k-1} e^{-(x/\lambda)^k} & x \geq 0, \\ 0 & x < 0, \end{cases}$$

Other Useful Distributions

There are a few distributions from attribute data. Binomial, Poisson, hypergeometric, are examples of that.

The Binomial Distribution

If we have a number of independent trials with only two possible outcomes: good vs bad, accept vs reject. Assuming the probability of success is constant, then number of successes follow the binomial distribution, in other words, we can calculate the probability of success in "n" trials. We discuss this further in the chapter for Sample Size Determination.

$$p(x) = \binom{n}{x} p^x (1-p)^{n-x}$$

Where x = 0,1,2..., n

Example

We know that we have a therapy that will cure 9 out of 10 patients. If we do an additional trial with another 10 patients. The probability that we have of curing exactly 7 patients in these last 10 trials is 5.7%, but It goes up to 38.7% when we cure exactly 9 patients. The cumulative probability of curing up to 9 patients, will be 65.13%.

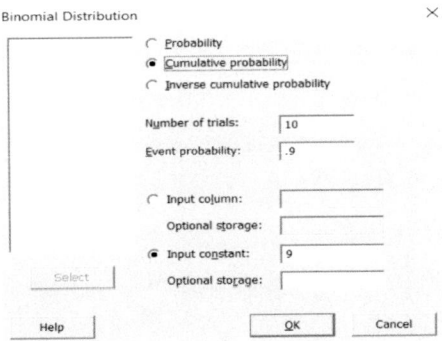

The Poisson Distribution

This distribution is useful to model the number of defects that occur in a unit of product, with the condition that this is a random phenomenon. If the defects are clustered, other distributions are more appropriate. We can also use this distribution to estimate the probability of rejection or acceptance of a production lot.

$$p(x) = \frac{e^{-\lambda} \lambda^x}{x!}$$

Where x = 1,2,3....

Example

The probability of finding a missing screw in a car is 0.02, if we inspect 100 cars, the probability of zero (0) defects in 100 cars is: 0.135 or 13.5%, and the probability of rejecting the production lot is: 86.5%.

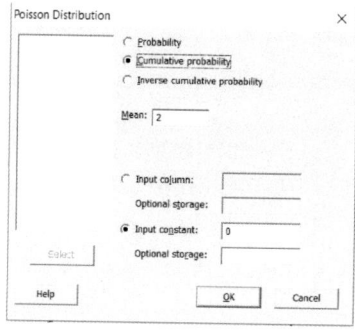

The "mean: 2" comes from calculating the average number of defects per 100 cars inspected: 100*0.02 = 2.

Hypergeometric Distribution

This distribution is useful in calculating the probability of finding a random nonconforming unit from a sample without replacement from a finite population. To calculate this probability, we need to know the size of the population "N", the size of the sample "n", and the number of nonconforming items "D").

$$p(x) = \frac{\binom{D}{x}\binom{N-D}{n-x}}{\binom{N}{n}}$$

Where x = 0,1,2,.... Min (n, D)

Fortunately, statistical software can do the calculation for us.

Example

Going back to the previous example, let's say we suspect that in 1 car out of 100 cars the engine doesn't work, and we already shipped 100 cars to each one of our dealers. If we were to sample 10 cars in every dealership, the proportion of all the accepted lots will be 90%.

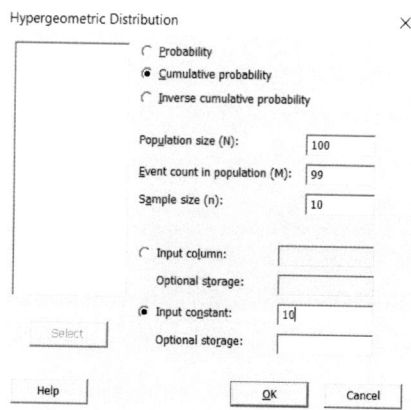

Statistical Process Control

Definition

Statistical process control refers to the identification of critical product specifications and monitoring of their behavior throughout the production process by means of statistical methods. The goal is to ensure that we have a stable process by reducing the variation that will affect the quality of the product, it's reliability, and cost.

A controlled process means that the process is stable and predictable. This way we ensure that:

1. The capability of the process is maintained and improved over time.
2. Variation is reduced.
3. Special causes of variation versus common cause of variation are identified.

A process is stable when the location, variation or spread, and the shape of the distribution remain constant over time.

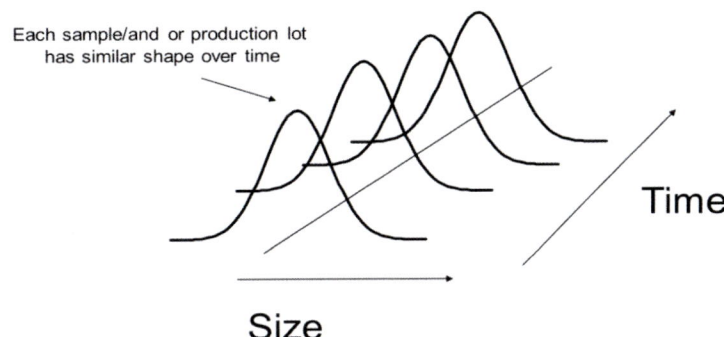

A common cause of variation is defined as a factor that contributes to regular everyday variation to our process, our goal is to reduce that variation.

A special cause of variation is defined as a factor that is not always present in our process but appears in a particular circumstance.

A process is said to be in statistical control when the process is not being affected by special causes of variation, and all the points fall within the control limits randomly dispersed around the average line.

Now, control charts are necessary to assess process stability. There are different control charts, and the application of these charts will depend on the type of data that we can collect form the process. We can have control charts for variable, and attribute data.

The following decision tree can aid you in identifying the different types of control charts applicable in industry environments:

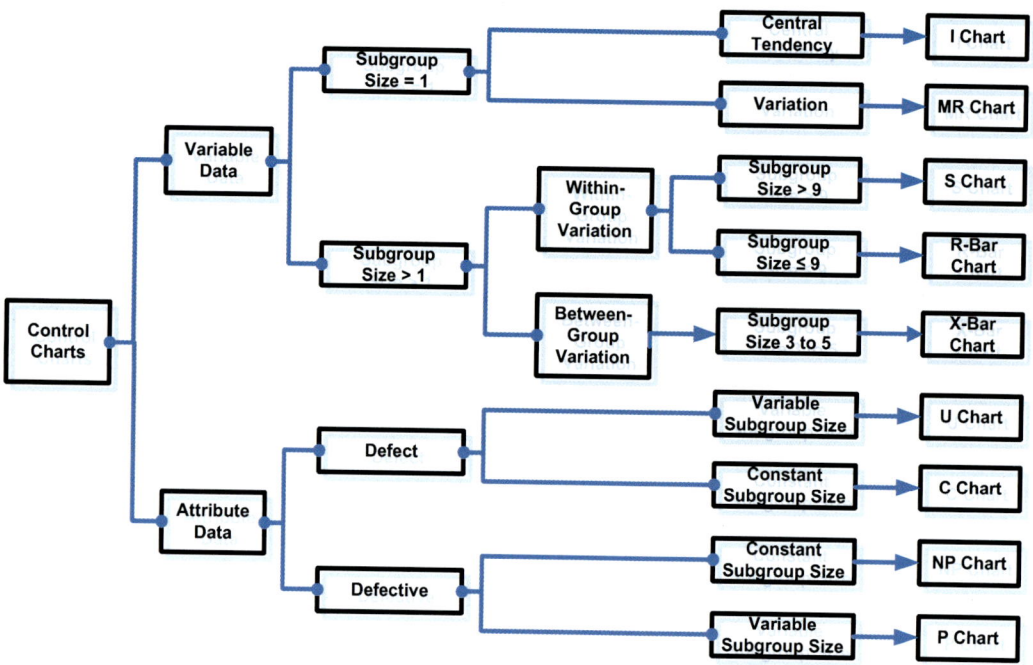

In this handbook we are mainly going to talk about the most common control charts for variable data: X bar, I, and R charts.

$\overline{x}$ (X-bar), Chart

X-bar chart is the most common chart in SPC. It can help us to detect process changes. However, it is not very sensitive to small or gradual changes over time.

The X-bar chart can detect changes in the process mean, and the out of control points indicate a shift in the process mean.

In this chart the control limits are calculated on the process variation – NOT THE SPECIFICATION LIMITS.

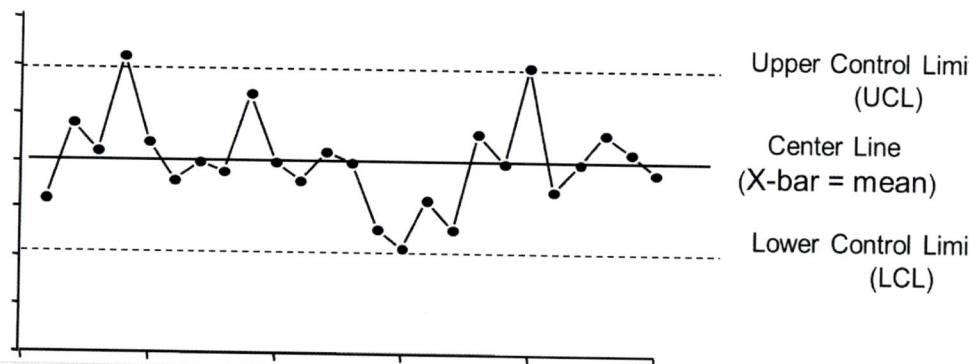

The points within the control limits reflect the common process variation and the stability of the process. The points falling out of the limits represent special causes of variation.

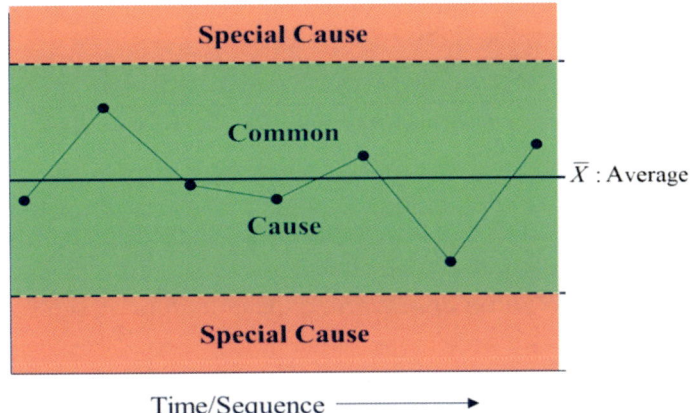

From the resulting graph, if we divide the chart in zones – at a sigma (σ) distance- according to the distance from the mean, we can get three different zones on each side of the X-bar.

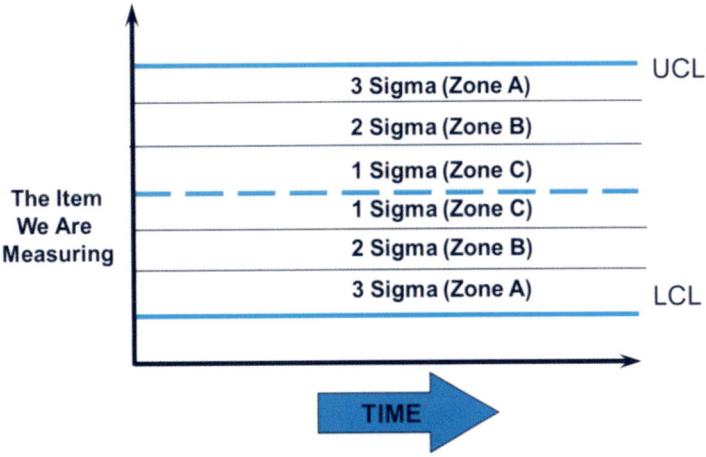

For control charts we can use the Western Electric/Nelson rules to determine if the process is out of control, these are the rules:

Test 1 - Any point outside control limits – zone A

Test 2 - 9 consecutive points on same side of centerline – zone C

Test 3 - 6 consecutive points increasing or decreasing

Test 4 - 14 consecutive points alternating up and down

Test 5 - 2 of 3 points in same zone A or beyond

Test 6 - 4 of 5 points in same zone B or beyond

Test 7 - 15 consecutive points in either zone C

Test 8 - 8 points in a row outside zone C, on either side of centerline

The values of an X-bar must come from rational subgrouping. The subgrouping, when done properly, will help us identify or segregate common causes of variation from special causes of variation. This is very important: if the subgrouping is done incorrectly, rather than helping us identify variation it could smooth the measurements so much that the chart won't detect enough variation and just seem under control, when in reality that is not the case.

The subgroups must be small, of a constant size, usually from 2 to 5 consecutive pieces, taken at a regular time interval, for example, every 30 minutes, three times per shift, etc. the number of subgroups should satisfy two basic requirements:

1. Enough subgroups must be collected to be able to identify major sources of variation. Usually, 25 or more subgroups give enough information for stability and spread. (after 25 subgroups we must re-calculate the limits).
2. Take samples under the same operating conditions, if the conditions of the process change, a new chart must be created.

Every time we initiate a control chart in a process with no previous data, we will not have control limits, and the chart must be plotted and identified as "Initial Study".

Example

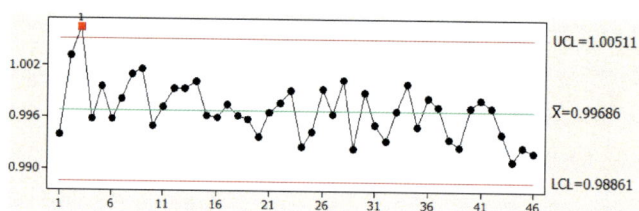

In this example the process breaks rule number one. Then, apparently someone adjusted the process to stabilize it, but by the end of the run, the process shows symptoms of a downward trend.

The whole point of a control chart is to identify the process behavior, we must pay attention to what the process chart is trying to tell us.

Note: To be technically correct, in the X-bar chart, the process average is actually:

$$\bar{\bar{X}}$$

this is also named as x-bar-bar.

The x-bar-bar depicts the average of the averages. Remember, each average corresponds to an individual subgroup and is therefore plotted as an individual value in the chart. Consequently, the lower and upper control limits are defined by:

$$LCL = \bar{\bar{X}} - 3\frac{\hat{\sigma}}{\sqrt{n}}$$

$$UCL = \bar{\bar{X}} + 3\frac{\hat{\sigma}}{\sqrt{n}}$$

I-Chart

In the "individuals" chart, we plot the individual values of our sample, not the average of a subgroup. In other words, our subgroup is equal to 1. The Western electric principles also apply to the I-charts, but the lower and upper control limits are 3 times the standard deviation on each direction:

- UCL = X-bar (data mean) + 3 σ
- LCL = X-bar - 3 σ

The I-charts are more sensitive than the x-bar charts and make it easier to detect changes in our process. This chart is especially useful in short production lots; if we are running a process with hundreds or thousands of data points (parts), I recommend the x-bar chart instead.

Example:

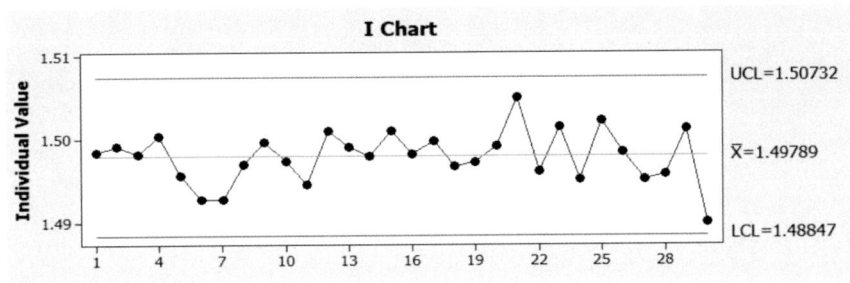

Can a process be under control and out of specification at the same time? the answer is: yes! The limits are calculated based on process variation, and not on the customer specifications.

Can the process be within customer specification and out of control? The answer is: yes! The customer specifications can be so wide that the process produces parts with out of control variation, but still under the customer requirements.

R-Chart

In the R-chart we follow the same idea of the x-bar, and I chart, but in this case, we plot the ranges between measurements. These charts are good to track process variation, but particularly special causes of variation.

In X-bar charts, R is defined as: $R = X_{highest} - X_{lowest}$ for each sub-group.

In I-charts the R is defined as: $R = X_{n+1} - X_n$, where "n" is defined as each individual value.

The range mean in the chart is defined as R-bar. See the next example:

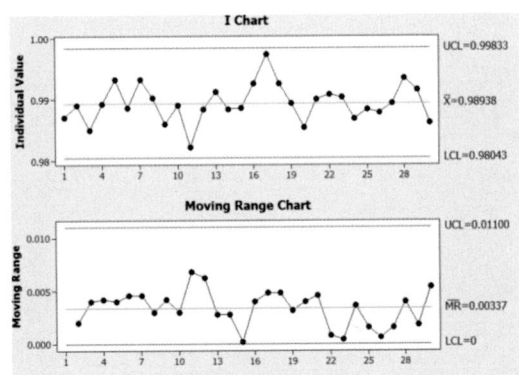

Control Chart for Attribute Data (P-Chart, NP-Chart)

Percent defective data can be tracked and analyzed through a P-Chart. In a P-Chart (control chart) we can plot the percent defective of samples over time. Even if the sample size changes occasionally, the control limits in the chart can be adjusted. For example, following the path: Stat>Control Charts>Attribute Charts>P or NP

This is an NP-Chart where the sample size is constant.

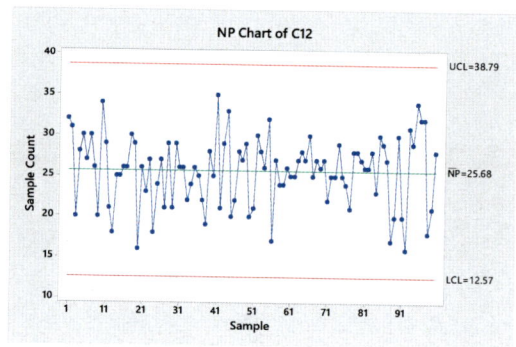

This is a P-Chart where the sample size changes:

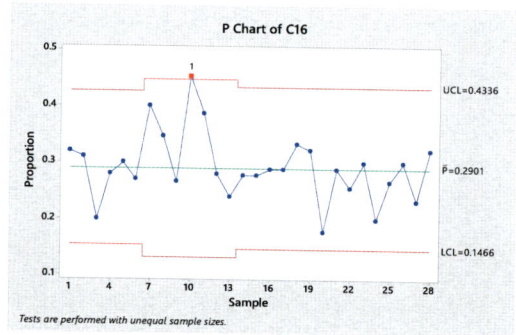

Control Chart for Attribute Data (U-Chart, C-Chart)

To monitor defects per opportunity (basically more than 1 defect per unit), we use the U-Chart for variable sample size and the C-Chart when sample size is constant.

This is an example of the U-Chart (variable sample size):

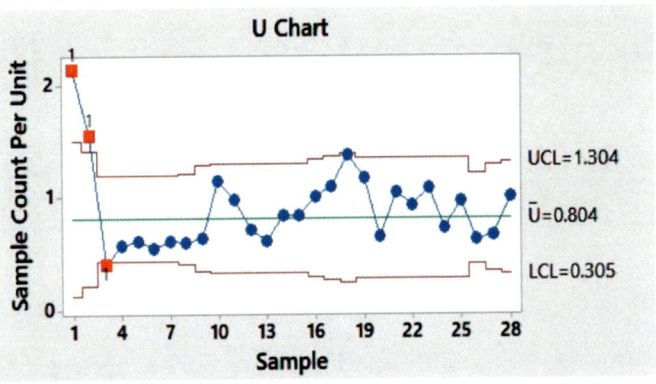

This is the C-Chart (constant sample size):

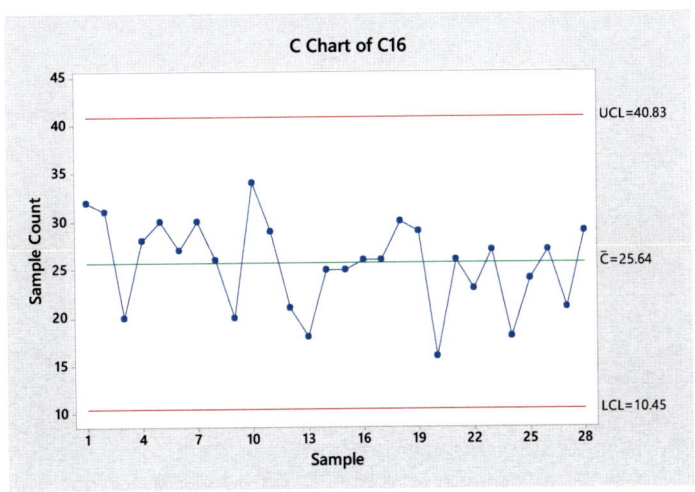

Process Capability for Variable and Attribute Data

Definition

Capability, for our purposes, will be defined as the ability of a process to meet the customer requirements (specifications). Therefore, we need specification limits to determine if our process (measured by the product characteristics) falls within the range or limits of the customer requirement.

The customer requirements are usually defined by an upper and lower specification limits.

Capability indices are defined by Cp, and Cpk, and calculated following these formulas:

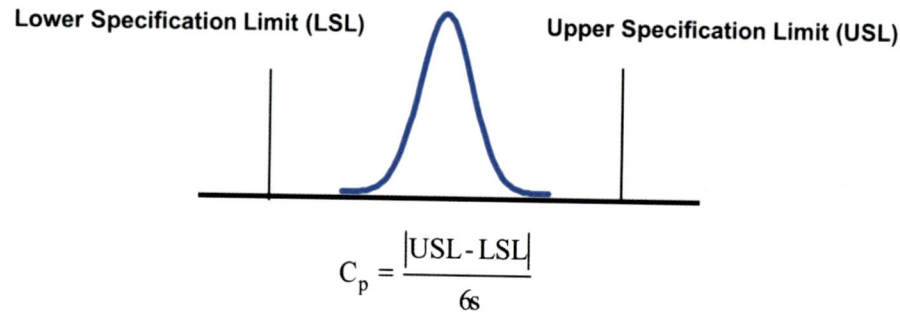

$$C_p = \frac{|USL - LSL|}{6s}$$

Cp is a good estimate of the entitlement of the process based on current process variation(s). But we need Cpk to estimate the actual process capability. To this end, we will first need to calculate Cpl and Cpu:

$$C_{pl} = \frac{\bar{X} - LSL}{3s} \qquad C_{pu} = \frac{USL - \bar{X}}{3s}$$

This is the formula for Cpk:

$$C_{pk} = Min(\frac{\bar{X} - LSL}{3s}, \frac{USL - \bar{X}}{3s})$$

Cpk is the minimum value from Cpl and Cpu

Note: For short term variation, S (within subgroup standard deviation) is calculated:

$$S = \bar{R}/d_2$$

Where d_2 is a number calculated based on the subgroup size --we need statistical tables for that. Fortunately, MINITAB (or any other statistical software) can do the calculation for us. Furthermore, there are other functions in MINITAB that will help us visualize the process based on our sample, like the "Capability Sixpack™".

Based on these formulas we can infer the following: we can calculate Cpk with just one specification limit, but no Cp. Cpk, measures the distance of the sample or process mean to the closest limit. If we want to know the distance of the sample/process mean to the target value (assuming the specification calls for a target value in our process), then we use the Cpm – MINITAB provides that for us too.

Based on the formulas we can see that the capability indices will improve as the standard deviation gets smaller and/or the specification limits get wider. Since the goal is not to change the customer specification, the standard deviation will have to get smaller. We can achieve that by reducing the process variation. This following graph shows how the variation or data spread will affect the shape of our process/curve:

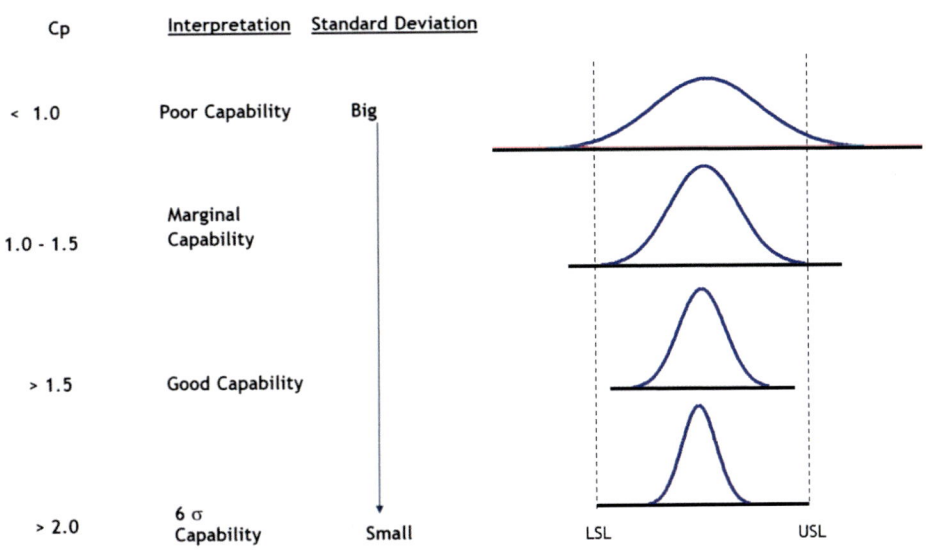

Important Note:

There are two basic requirements that we need to meet in order to have a meaningful capability index:

1. The process must be normally distributed (it must follow a normal distribution). Otherwise, in order to be able to calculate capability, you will first need to identify the distribution and then calculate the capability for that specific distribution – MINITAB can do that for you. Another option is to transform the data, to make it normal, but we need to be careful before we make these decisions, because sometimes the lack of normality may be caused by the measurement system and special causes of variation that do not represent the regular process. Throughout the years, I have seen capability results being affected by the wrong measurement system, operator error, shift changes, wrong sample collection, segregation, and special causes of process variation. We must discard all these factors before we proceed with our analysis.

2. The process must be under statistical process control, that means that the process must be stable and predictable.

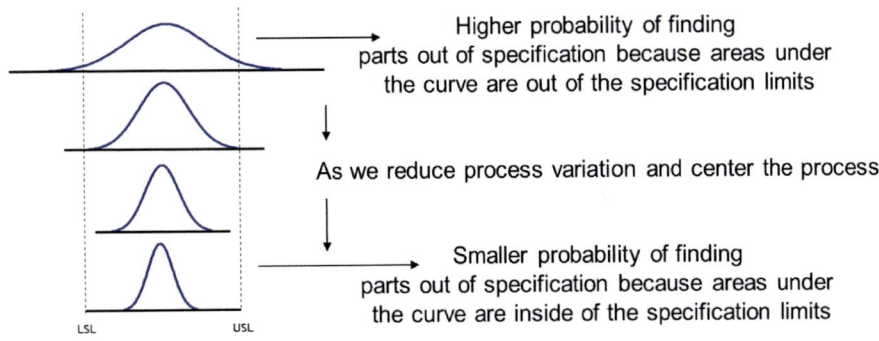

Example of good capability:

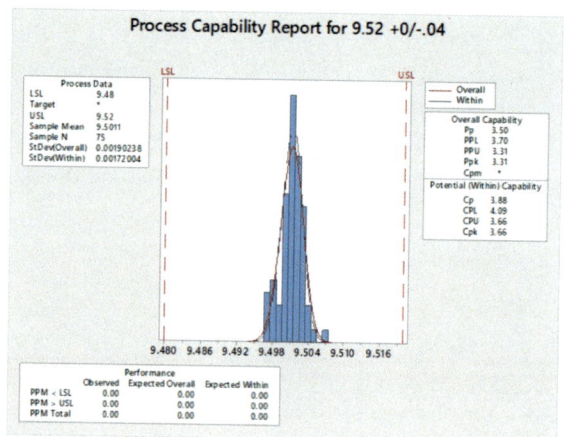

Example of good capability – Sixpack:

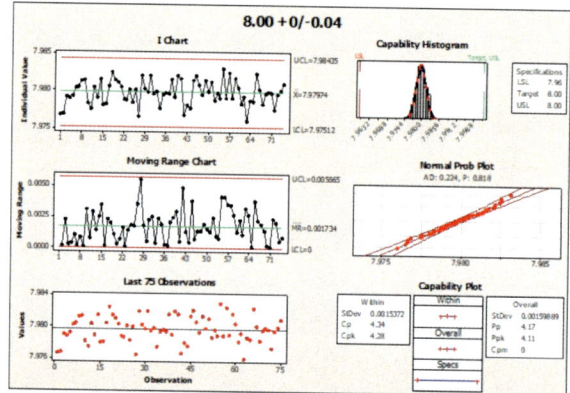

In this example, the I-Chart shows that the process is under statistical control, and the normal probability plot shows that the process is normally distributed.

Example of bad capability:

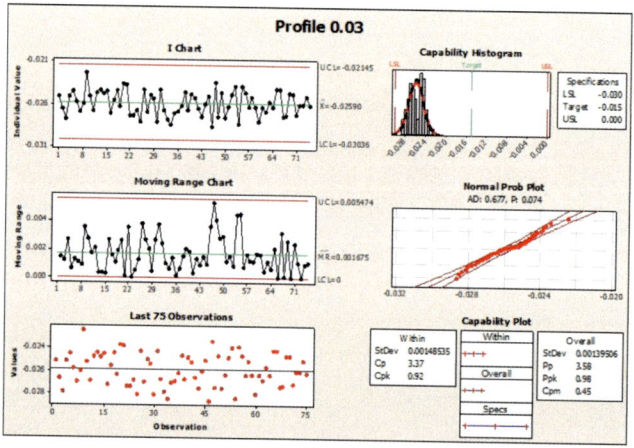

In this example the process meets the two basic requirements, but it is too close to the lower specification limit, having a low Cpk (under 1.0) and the potential of parts being out of specification on the lower side (defective parts). If we re-run the capability analysis - not the capability Sixpack- we get the following chart:

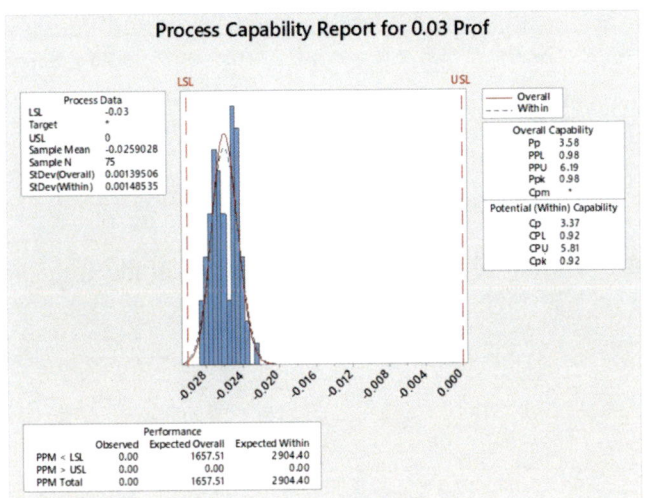

The analysis clearly shows that we can potential have 1,657 parts out of specification for every million parts we produce.

One last example:

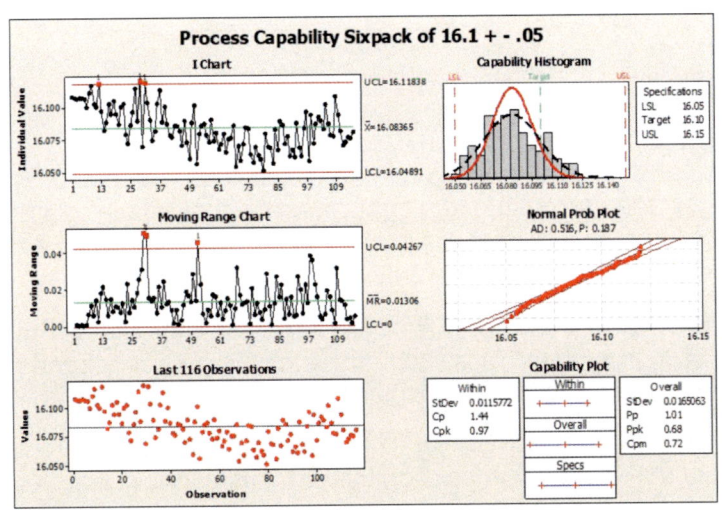

In this chart we can see that the process is clearly out of control (I-chart), the process was moving from the upper specification towards the lower specification and then, apparently, the process was adjusted towards the target specification. Therefore, the analysis must be repeated from scratch with the required adjustment.

Pp and Ppk (Process Performance index) – Short Term vs Long Term Capability

Cp and Cpk are usually named "short term capability" while Pp and Ppk are usually called "long term capability". To calculate Pp and Ppk we use the same formulas that we used for Cp and Cpk, so, what's the difference? The difference is in the standard deviation: for Cp and Cpk we use the statistic "s" based on subgroups and for Pp and Ppk we use the overall process variation estimated by:

$$s = \sqrt{\frac{\sum(x - \bar{x})^2}{n - 1}}$$

This is the overall variation in the process including shifts and drifts, while the "s" in Cp and Cpk is calculated based on variation within subgroups as I mentioned before.

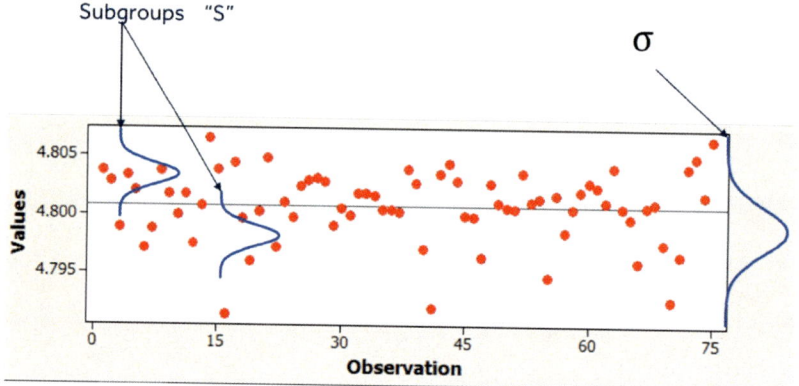

When calculating Cp and Cpk, the "s" is estimated based on rational subgroups (the formulas include the average of ranges and the values from subgroup size that require statistical tables), while in Pp and Ppk "σ" is calculated based on the formula in chapter 1. MINITAB or any other statistical software does this for us and we don't have to manually calculate these numbers.

In the previous examples we can see that MINITAB also provides Pp and Ppk when calculating capability. The application and use of these indices in real life will depend on the requirements of each quality system as established by that particular company.

Going back to the subject of distribution identification, the following example shows how identifying the shape of the process may have an impact on the process capability, in this case the Pp and Ppk.

In the following graph we can see the Capability Sixpack for a sample that is not normally distributed. The Pp= 2.19 and the Ppk=2.11, so we could say has good long term capability. However, from the graph it is clear that the process has outliers in the I-chart and a moving range chart, which is not good:

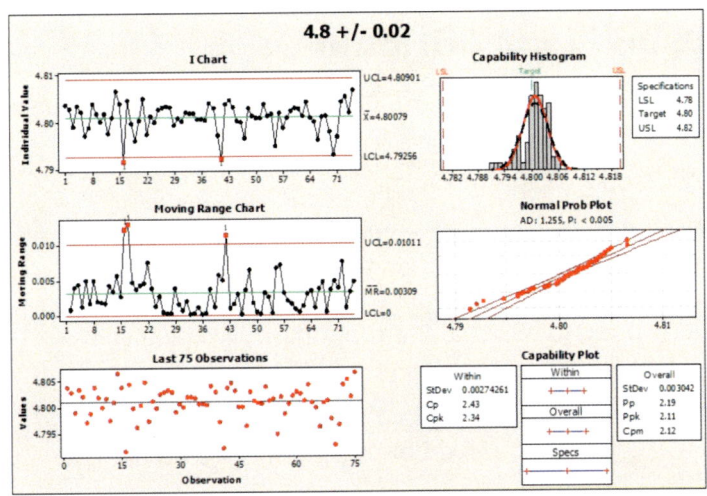

Given that the data is clearly not normally distributed, someone may be inclined to disregard the theoretical requirements for a meaningful process capability and accept these Pp, and Ppk values as true. DON'T! This would have consequences in the quality of the product going out of production. Why? Because in many cases, the process capability determines the inspection level of the final product.

Now, let's assume for a moment that this process actually follows a different distribution (in this case lognormal), and calculate the process capability following the lognormal distribution using the MINITAB Capability Sixpack for non-normal distribution. This is what we get:

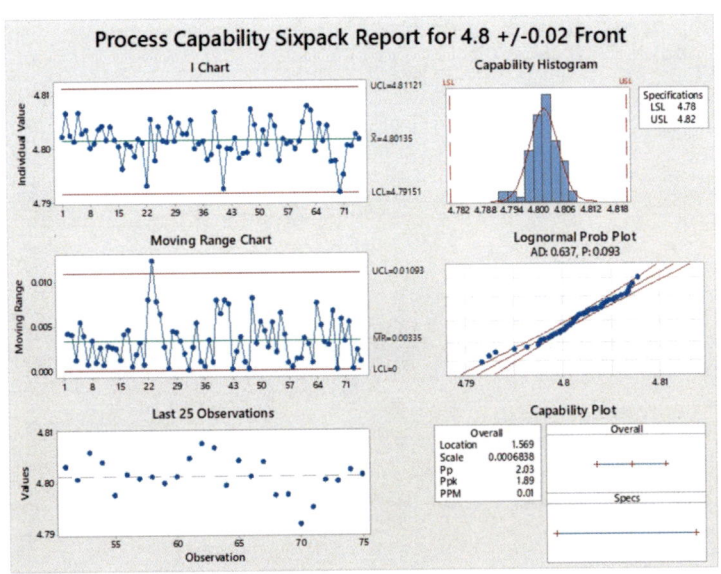

Under a lognormal distribution, the process seems to be mostly under control, and the long term capability, Ppk, is 1.89, not 2.11 as we previously calculated. This is relatively a small difference in Ppk --I have seen bigger differences in similar situations while calculating process capabilities--, but as evidenced in the rest of the charts this is clearly more appropriate result to use.

Process Capability for Attribute Data

As we mentioned before, data can be variable or attribute. There is also a way to calculate process capability for attribute data.

For the proportion of defective parts/products:

% Defective = $\dfrac{\text{Number of defective parts in the sample}}{\text{Number of parts inspected/sample}}$ X 100

A common terminology used to express the proportion of defective parts is: defective parts per million (DPM):

(DPM) Defective parts per million = $\dfrac{\text{Number of defective parts in the sample}}{\text{Number of parts inspected/sample}}$ X 1,000,000

(DPU) Defects per unit = $\dfrac{\text{Total of defects found}}{\text{Number of parts inspected}}$

(DPMO) Defects per million opportunities = $\dfrac{\text{Number of defects found in the sample}}{\text{Number of opportunities inspected}}$ X 1,000,000

For attribute data, MINITAB provides the option to calculate the capability of the data as "Binomial". Binomial means that there are only two possible outcomes: good vs bad.

Example:

If we collect 100 samples of 100 units each, and we count the number of defective units for each sample, we can get a graphical output of the process behavior using the Binomial distribution. The path is: Stat>Quality Tools>Capability Analysis>Binomial

This is the resulting graph:

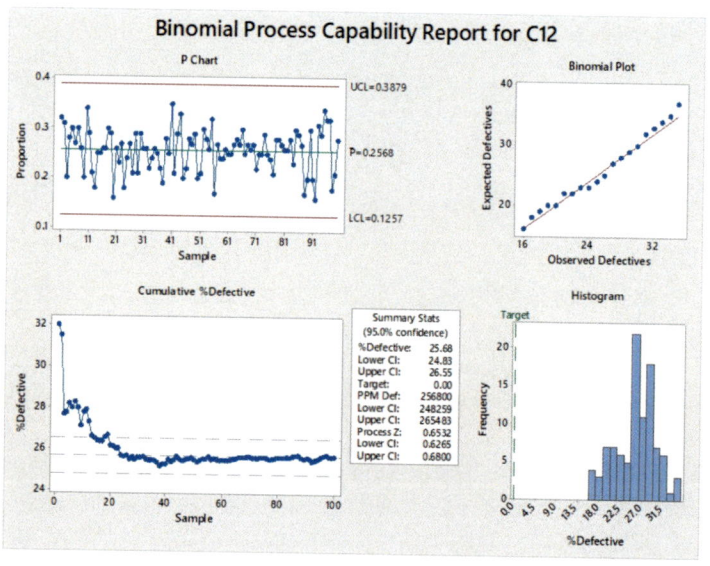

The results show that the percent defective is 25.68%, with a 95% confidence interval of (24.83%, 26.55%) --more about this in the confidence interval chapter--. In this output we also get the same results in PPM (parts per million). The P chart shows that our process is under control and the Binomial Plot shows that our process follows the corresponding binomial distribution.

The nice thing about the P chart, is that if the sample size changes from sample to sample, the control limits change accordingly.

If we want to calculate the DPU (defect per million opportunities), we follow the Poisson distribution. The path is: Stat>Quality Tools>Capability Analysis>Poisson

Example:

We take 28 samples of different sizes and we assess the number of defects of each part in the sample. When applying the Poisson distribution we get:

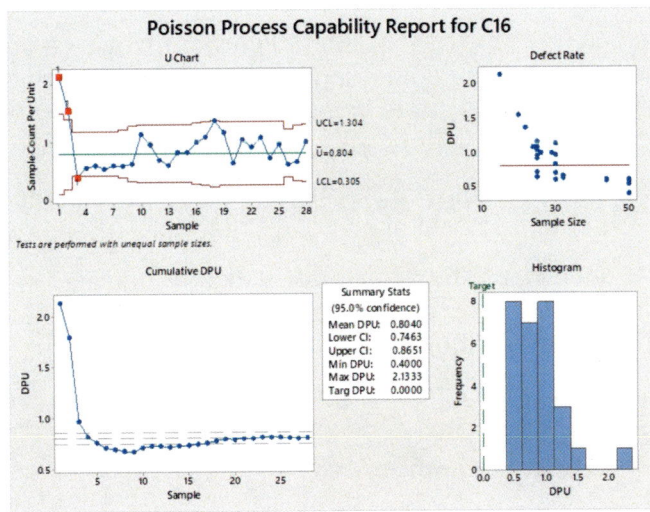

Notice how the control limits in the U Chart change according to the sample size. The estimated defects per unit is: 0.804 with a 95% confidence interval of (0.7463, 0.8651).

Measurement System Analysis

In previous chapters we discussed statistical process control and process capability, but the validity of our analysis and all our results depends directly on the measurement system that produced the data. The main purpose of the measurement system analysis is to determine if said measurement system is suitable for it's intended purpose.

For example, we can have the best calibrated caliper that we can get in the industry, but this caliper is not the best measuring tool for some applications. Furthermore, the way we use the caliper and the circumstances surrounding the measurements will also affect the final data collected. We are talking of all the conditions involved and surrounding the measurement collection, including the operators.

In any measurement system, the results are defined by the accuracy and precision of the measurement system. In a measurement system analysis, we determine the "precision" of our measurement system.

Precision can be defined as the amount of variation between measurements. While "bias" can be defined as the difference between the true value and the average of repeated measurements. Hence, "accuracy" can be defined as the lack of bias.

The following chart shows the difference between accuracy and precision:

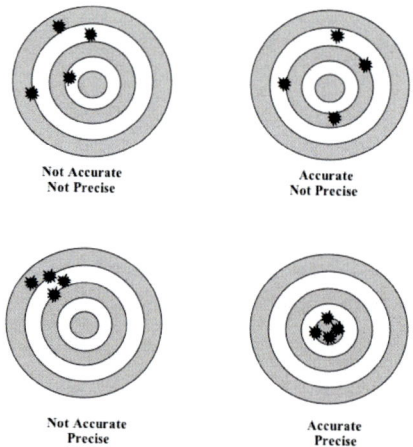

If we take multiple measurements of a defined characteristic and we plot the results (assuming normal distribution), we will get something like this:

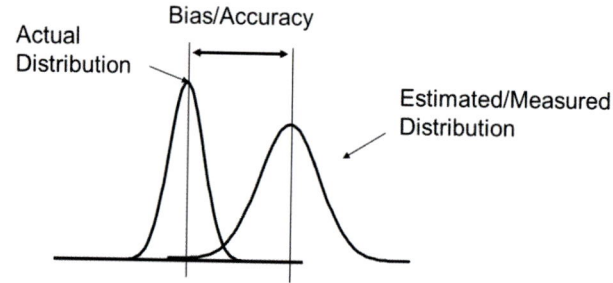

Therefore, if we don't have a good measurement system we increase the chance of misclassifying a bad part as acceptable, or, rejecting a good part misclassifying it as a bad part. As we improve the precision of our measurement system, the chance of miss-classification is reduced, hence rendering a better process outcome. The following chart illustrates that.

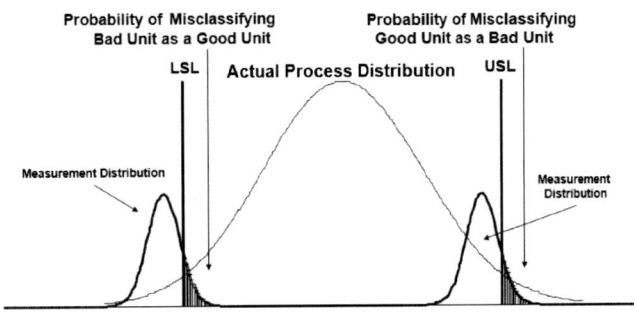

We need to quantify the error (variation) in the measurement system and classify it into one of the following four different categories: repeatability, reproducibility, stability, and bias. We already defined bias, these are the other definitions:

- Repeatability is defined as the variation in the measurements when the same part is measured with the same measuring device by the same operator.
- Reproducibility is defined as the variation in the average of measurements when the characteristic is measured with the same device by different operators.
- Stability is defined as the amount of variation in the measurements for a single characteristic over time, compared to a standard.

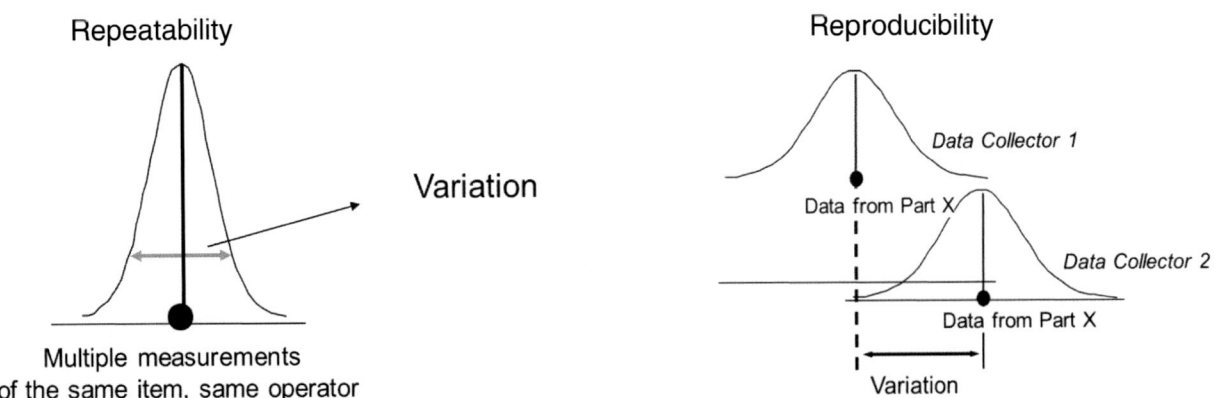

Types of Measurement System Analysis

There are three basic – and most common – types of measurement system analysis:

1. Variable MSA: Usually Crossed Gage R&R or ANOVA
2. Destructive MSA: Usually Nested Gage R&R
3. Attribute MSA: Also called "Attribute R&R", and also known as "Attribute Agreement Analysis"

To minimize the operator bias in the measurement analysis, there are some conditions or recommendations that will guarantee a reliable R&R result:

1. Operators must measure parts in random order
2. Operators should not know the actual number of the part to be measured

3. Parts and operators must be representative of the actual process
4. Use parts that represent the width of the total tolerance or specification – this is eventually a factor for what is called "part-to-part variation"
5. Write down the measurement method and train operators to ensure consistency on the measurement system

Resolution

We can find different definitions for resolution, but for our purposes it will be defined as the ability to place the measured values into multiple categories. It is applied to the gage or measuring device that will be used in our measurement system. The recommendation is that we use a gage/measuring device with a resolution that is at least 1/10th of the total specification (range of tolerance) that will be measured, This is: (USL-LSL)/10.

Variable R&R (non-destructive)

Ideally the variable R&R study must include 3 operators, 10 parts, 3 repeats (each operator will measure the same part 3 times). It makes a total of 90 measurements.

Sometimes, due to time and resource limitations the R&R study must be minimized, if this is the case the lowest number of measurements allowed is 20, as long as we need to estimate repeatability and reproducibility.

To have 20 measurements we must have at least 2 operators, 5 parts, 2 repeats.

This is the acceptance criteria for variable R&R results:

	Good	Use with Caution	Danger (Do not use)
P/T Ratio (Precision to Tolerance ratio)	< 10%	10% to 30%	>30%
Gage R&R (study variation)	< 10%	10% to 30%	>30%
% Contribution	< 2%	2% to 7.7%	>7.7%
Number of Distinct Categories	> 10	5 to 10	< 5

The gage R&R result (or study variation) is based on the ratio of 2 standard deviations, while the percent (%) contribution is based on the ratio of two variances. The industry has been using the percent (%) study variation for several years and it is basically the industry standard to determine gage R&R – probably because it is easier to understand compared to other criteria--, but the percent contribution is also statistically valid.

Before we go into an example let's visualize the variation and its sources. The total variation is the result of:

$$\hat{\sigma}^2_{Total\ Variation} = \hat{\sigma}^2_{Product\ (part\ to\ part)} + \underbrace{\hat{\sigma}^2_{Measurement\ System}}_{\underbrace{\hat{\sigma}^2_{Repeatability} + \hat{\sigma}^2_{Reproducibility}}_{\hat{\sigma}^2_{Due\ to\ Operators} + \hat{\sigma}^2_{Due\ to\ operator\ to\ part\ interaction}}}$$

Example:

In this example we will take measurements on two different product characteristics, t2 and t1_1. If we did a gage R&R study with only 20 measurements our table may look like this.

C2	C3	C4	C5	C6
Op No	Trial No	Part No	t2	t1_1
1	1	1	9.9715	10.0436
1	1	2	10.0153	10.0104
1	1	3	9.9982	9.9914
1	1	4	10.0503	10.0599
1	1	5	10.0069	10.0070
1	2	1	9.9744	10.0425
1	2	2	10.0177	10.0214
1	2	3	9.9968	10.0123
1	2	4	10.0479	10.0585
1	2	5	10.0053	10.0081
2	1	1	9.9704	10.0462
2	1	2	10.0172	10.0345
2	1	3	9.9962	10.0027
2	1	4	10.0534	10.0598
2	1	5	10.0023	10.0168
2	2	1	9.9730	10.0393
2	2	2	10.0185	10.0194
2	2	3	10.0004	10.0086
2	2	4	10.0546	10.0518
2	2	5	10.0075	10.0204

The MINITAB sequence for variable R&R is: Stat>Quality Tools>Gage Study> Gage R&R Study (Crossed).

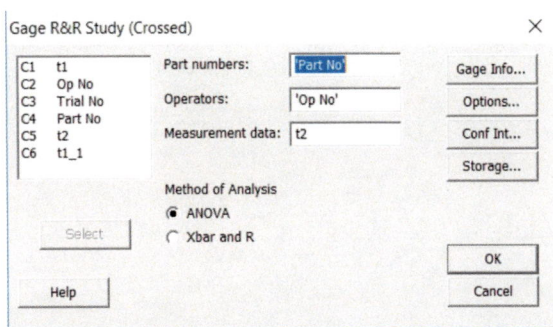

Identify the part numbers, operators, and measurement data and select "Options":

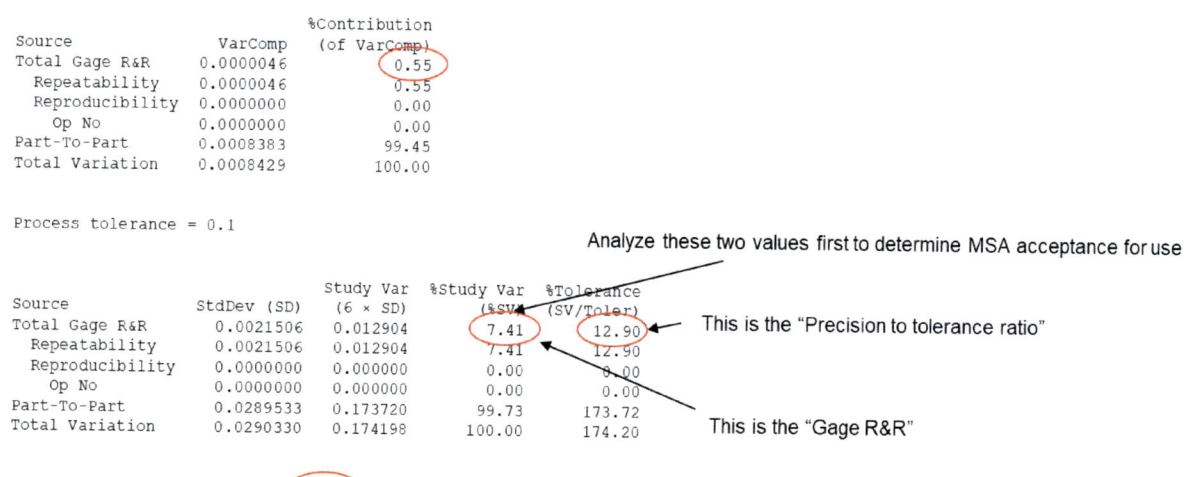

Then, enter the total process tolerance (specification width), or alternately, each value for lower and upper specification limits. After clicking "OK" in both windows, we will get this information in the session window:

Two-Way ANOVA Table Without Interaction

```
Source          DF    SS         MS         F         P
Part No          4    0.0134312  0.0033578  725.975   0.000
Op No            1    0.0000042  0.0000042    0.915   0.355
Repeatability   14    0.0000648  0.0000046
Total           19    0.0135001
```

Gage R&R

```
                                      %Contribution
Source              VarComp           (of VarComp)
Total Gage R&R      0.0000046          0.55
  Repeatability     0.0000046          0.55
  Reproducibility   0.0000000          0.00
    Op No           0.0000000          0.00
Part-To-Part        0.0008383         99.45
Total Variation     0.0008429        100.00

Process tolerance = 0.1

                                 Study Var    %Study Var    %Tolerance
Source              StdDev (SD)  (6 × SD)     (%SV)         (SV/Toler)
Total Gage R&R      0.0021506    0.012904       7.41          12.90
  Repeatability     0.0021506    0.012904       7.41          12.90
  Reproducibility   0.0000000    0.000000       0.00           0.00
    Op No           0.0000000    0.000000       0.00           0.00
Part-To-Part        0.0289533    0.173720      99.73         173.72
Total Variation     0.0290330    0.174198     100.00         174.20

Number of Distinct Categories = 18
```

Analyze these two values first to determine MSA acceptance for use — 7.41 and 12.90. This is the "Precision to tolerance ratio". This is the "Gage R&R".

This is the amount of categories that the MSA can discriminate that are at least one confidence interval apart.

The number of distinct categories is calculated this way:

Number of categories = $\dfrac{\text{StdDev part-to-part}}{\text{Total GR\&R (first column)}} \times 1.41$

In this case: (0.0289533/0.0021506) X 1.41 = 18.98

The gage R&R of our MSA is 7.41% which represents the percentage of variation in our measurement system. If the gage R&R is large, only large shifts in the process can be detected. In this case, the value is under 10%, therefore our measurement system is acceptable.

The precision to tolerance ratio is 12.90%, meaning this is the percentage of the tolerance/specification being used by the above variation in the measurement system. Large p/t rations mean more risk of rejecting good parts or accepting bad ones, as we illustrated in previous graphs. This value is very useful in manufacturing processes because it provides an indication of the amount of variation in the measurement system as compared to the product specification and may help justify low process capability. In this example, the value of 12.9% is acceptable with caution, due to the tight tolerance (0.1).

If we use the same data with a different (wider) tolerance, then the p/t will be lower but that is not the case for either the R&R or the number of distinct categories. For example, let's assume the tolerance is 0.5 instead of 0.1 for the same measurement system. Then the results would be:

```
Gage R&R
                                  %Contribution
Source               VarComp      (of VarComp)
Total Gage R&R       0.0000046           0.55
  Repeatability      0.0000046           0.55
  Reproducibility    0.0000000           0.00
    Op No            0.0000000           0.00
Part-To-Part         0.0008383          99.45
Total Variation      0.0008429         100.00


Process tolerance = 0.5


                                Study Var    %Study Var   %Tolerance
Source              StdDev (SD)  (6 × SD)       (%SV)     (SV/Toler)
Total Gage R&R       0.0021506   0.012904         7.41         2.58
  Repeatability      0.0021506   0.012904         7.41         2.58
  Reproducibility    0.0000000   0.000000         0.00         0.00
    Op No            0.0000000   0.000000         0.00         0.00
Part-To-Part         0.0289533   0.173720        99.73        34.74
Total Variation      0.0290330   0.174198       100.00        34.84


Number of Distinct Categories = 18
```

The R&R and the number of distinct categories doesn't change, because we didn't change our measurement system (same data), but the p/t is now 2.58% because the tolerance is wider. One more thing: we can get the R&R even without a tolerance (because they are independent from each other). For example:

```
Gage R&R
                                  %Contribution
Source               VarComp      (of VarComp)
Total Gage R&R       0.0000046           0.55
  Repeatability      0.0000046           0.55
  Reproducibility    0.0000000           0.00
    Op No            0.0000000           0.00
Part-To-Part         0.0008383          99.45
Total Variation      0.0008429         100.00


                                Study Var    %Study Var
Source              StdDev (SD)  (6 × SD)       (%SV)
Total Gage R&R       0.0021506   0.012904         7.41
  Repeatability      0.0021506   0.012904         7.41
  Reproducibility    0.0000000   0.000000         0.00
    Op No            0.0000000   0.000000         0.00
Part-To-Part         0.0289533   0.173720        99.73
Total Variation      0.0290330   0.174198       100.00


Number of Distinct Categories = 18
```

Gage R&R for t2

As you can see, both, the R&R and the number of distinct categories, are there, but no p/t because we didn't provide a tolerance.

If we ran the same analysis for the second column of data t1_1, these would be the results:

Gage R&R

```
                                    %Contribution
Source              VarComp         (of VarComp)
Total Gage R&R      0.0000514        9.77
  Repeatability     0.0000462        8.77
  Reproducibility   0.0000052        1.00
    Op No           0.0000052        1.00
Part-To-Part        0.0004749       90.23
Total Variation     0.0005264      100.00

Process tolerance = 0.1

                                 Study Var    %Study Var   %Tolerance
Source              StdDev (SD)  (6 × SD)       (%SV)      (SV/Toler)
Total Gage R&R      0.0071707    0.043024       31.25        43.02
  Repeatability     0.0067956    0.040773       29.62        40.77
  Reproducibility   0.0022888    0.013733        9.98        13.73
    Op No           0.0022888    0.013733        9.98        13.73
Part-To-Part        0.0217931    0.130759       94.99       130.76
Total Variation     0.0229425    0.137655      100.00       137.66

Number of Distinct Categories = 4
```

In this example, the gage R&R is 31.25%, p/t is 43.02%, and 4 is the number of distinct categories. Based on our acceptance criteria table, this measurement system is not acceptable. Furthermore, the variation of the measurement system is using a whole 43% of our tolerance.

Graphical Output

MINITAB will also provide this chart every time we run an R&R study:

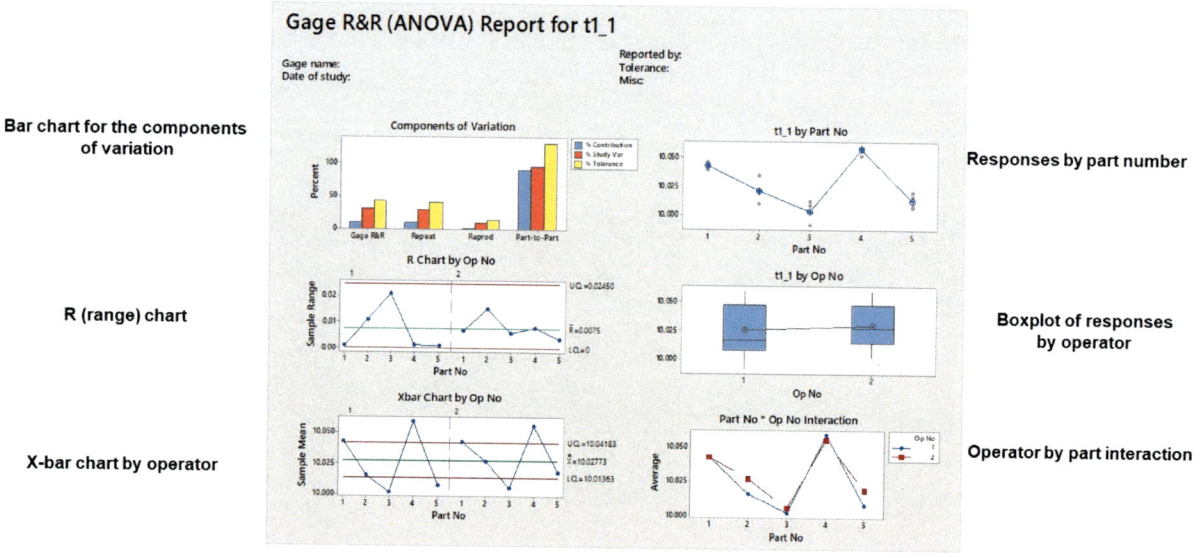

Let's now analyze each one of the charts in the graphical outcome:

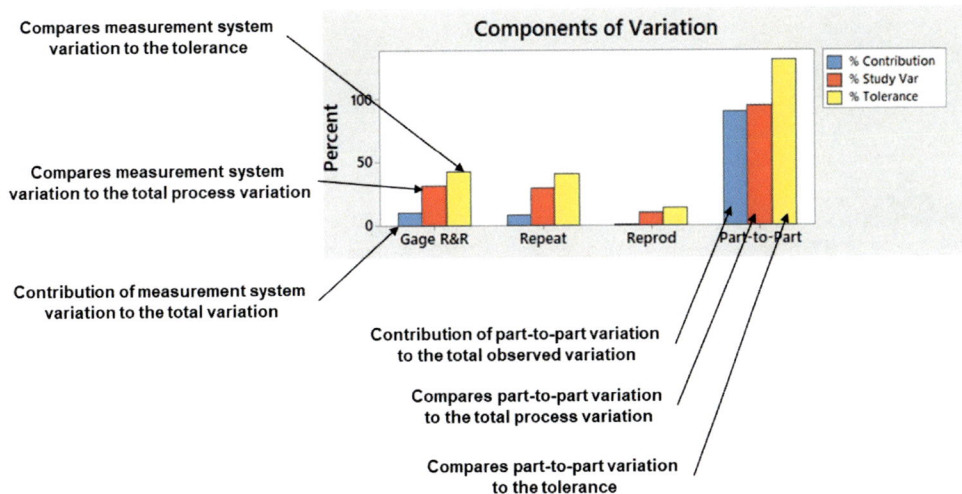

Ideally, most of the variability should be caused by part-to-part variation and not by the gage R&R. A high part-to-part variation is necessary to have a good gage R&R result. The part to part variation will depend on the selection of parts for the study. If the parts are selected consecutively from the same production run, chances are they will have small part to part variation, hence a high/bad R&R result, independently of the p/t ratio.

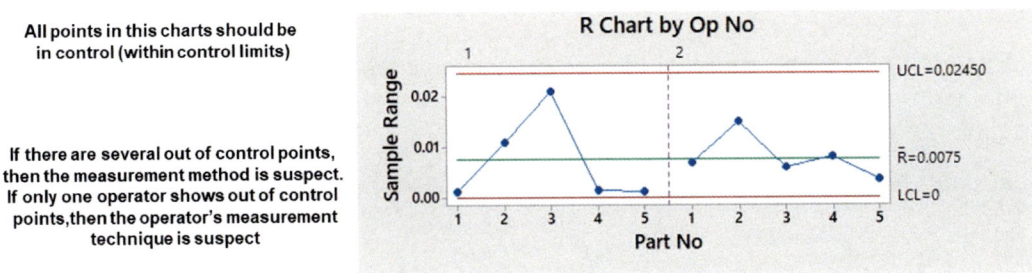

When analyzing this chart, if it shows mostly "0" values, the resolution of the gage may be suspect.

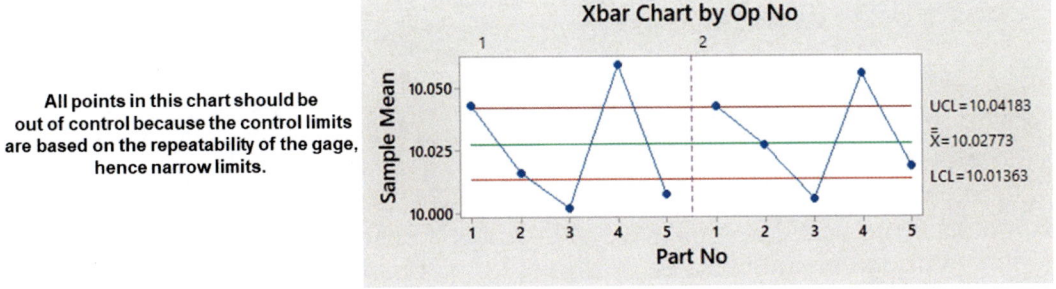

In this case, we want to see variation between parts (part-to-part variation), so most points should be out of control in this X-bar-bar chart. We should also see a similar pattern from operator to operator, as shown in this chart.

The next plot shows each individual measurement by part number and the average of the measurements for each part.

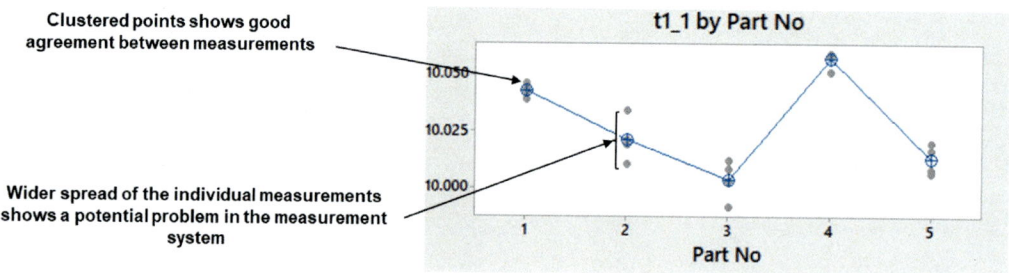

The "Y" axis must reflect the typical range of the process to be measured.

The next plot shows the boxplots of measurements by operator.

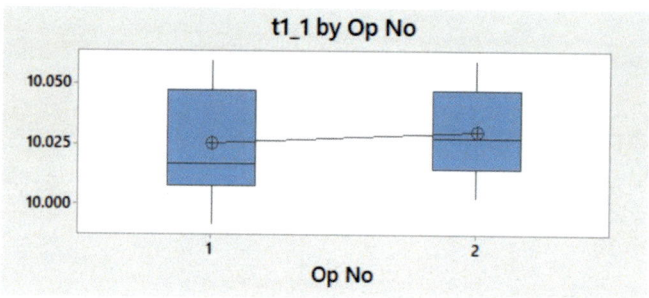

In the above chart we can visualize the difference and spread of measurements between operators. Given all boxes must look similar, the line connecting the boxes must be mostly horizontal: this line links the average values of each operator.

The next chart shows the part numbers on the "x" axis, and the different lines represent the different operators.

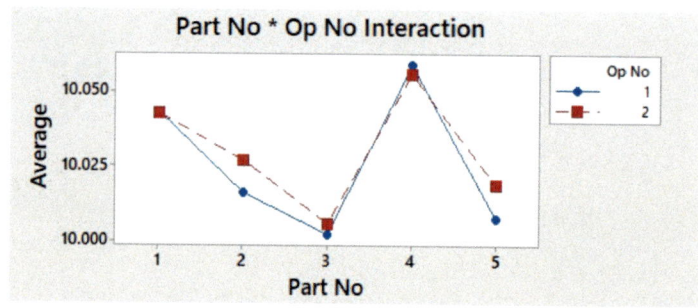

In this last chart we would want all lines to be superimposed. Where the lines move away from each other we see disagreement between operators for that particular part number. In this example that is what is happening with part numbers 2 and 5.

Note: So far, we have explained the ANOVA method of analysis, which I recommend; the X-Bar and the R method is more lenient because it doesn't take into consideration the significant factor of operator by part interactions.

Destructive Variable Gage R&R Study

Sometimes to measure a product characteristic -- For example: torque limit, strength resistance, pressure limits, etc.-- we have to destroy the part/product partially or totally. When this occurs, the same sample/part number can't be replicated, but we still can perform a gage R&R.

To perform a destructive variable R&R we need to use the "nested" method. This is similar to the regular variable R&R but the samples have to be replaced with new ones every time we perform the test. Take for example the case in the previous section: following the rule of a minimum of "20" measurements, instead of using 5 parts measured 2 times for each operator (minimum 2 operators), we will use a total of 20 parts. We need to make the assumption that the parts are identical enough that each and all would pass as the same part, otherwise the part-to-part variation within the lot will mask the measurement system variation.

The MINITAB path for this study is: Stat>Quality Tools>Gage Study>Gage R&R Study (Nested)

And the results are as follows:

Gage R&R

```
                                    %Contribution
Source              VarComp         (of VarComp)
Total Gage R&R      0.0000475               9.11
  Repeatability     0.0000475               9.11
  Reproducibility   0.0000000               0.00
Part-To-Part        0.0004735              90.89
Total Variation     0.0005210             100.00


                                    Study Var      %Study Var
Source              StdDev (SD)     (6 × SD)       (%SV)
Total Gage R&R      0.0068905       0.041343        30.19
  Repeatability     0.0068905       0.041343        30.19
  Reproducibility   0.0000000       0.000000         0.00
Part-To-Part        0.0217596       0.130558        95.33
Total Variation     0.0228245       0.136947       100.00


Number of Distinct Categories = 4
```

Even though we have the same data set, we don't have reproducibility (with the previous method reproducibility was 9.98%). In the nested R&R study, there is no calculated variation for the same part by different operators.

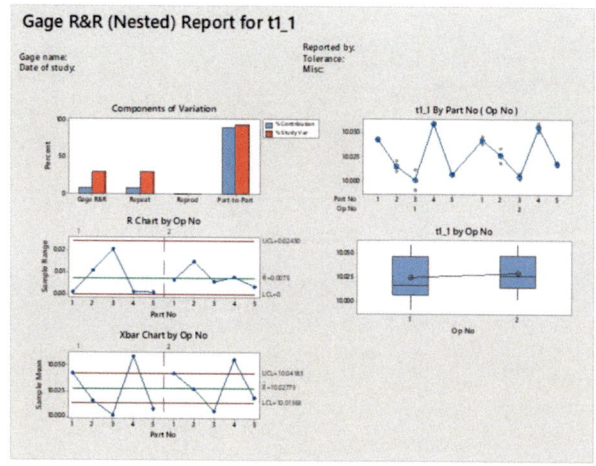

There is, obviously, no operator to part number interaction chart in the graphical outcome.

For destructive R&R studies, the acceptance criteria remain the same as the non-destructive R&R studies.

Attribute R&R Study

The purpose of this analysis is to quantify the percentage of agreement between appraisers, and the appraisers against a standard. This analysis pertains to the assessment of attribute characteristics like: colors, good vs bad, visual inspections, go vs no-go gages, etc.

This study is usually performed with 2 or 3 operators/inspectors, and one more person to coordinate the study. Typically, we need 30 or more parts, but I have seen studies with as few as 20 parts too (typically when the cost associated to the parts is high).

To eliminate bias, there are some conditions that need to be met for this analysis:

1. Each part must be labeled or identified with a number, identification must not be visible to the appraisers
2. Each appraiser assesses each part at least twice in random order
3. Appraisers must not know the number or identification of the part being assessed, only the coordinator of the study knows the identification and sequence of the parts
4. Only the study coordinator knows which parts are good or bad against a standard or expert appraiser
5. At least 20% of the parts must be bad parts

Example:

We will do an analysis for 24 parts, 3 appraisers, 3 trials, for a go / no-go gage, to determine the percent agreement among inspectors and compared to a standard, after collecting the data the spreadsheet would look something like this, (but you can stack up the columns too):

	C1-T	C2-T	C3-T	C4-T	C5-T	C6-T	C7-T	C8-T	C9-T	C10-T
	Standard	Appraiser1-1	Appraiser1-2	Appraiser1-3	Appraiser2-1	Appraiser2-2	Appraiser2-3	Appraiser3-1	Appraiser3-2	Appraiser3-3
1	P	P	P	P	P	P	P	P	P	P
2	F	F	F	F	F	F	F	F	F	F
3	F	F	F	F	F	F	F	F	F	F
4	P	P	P	P	P	P	P	P	P	P
5	P	P	P	P	P	P	P	P	P	P
6	F	F	F	F	F	F	F	F	F	F
7	F	F	F	F	F	F	F	F	F	F
8	P	P	P	P	P	P	P	P	P	P
9	P	P	P	P	P	P	P	P	P	P
10	P	P	P	P	P	P	P	P	P	P
11	F	F	F	F	F	F	F	F	F	F
12	P	P	P	P	P	P	P	P	P	P
13	F	F	F	F	F	F	F	F	F	F
14	P	P	P	P	F	P	P	P	P	P
15	P	P	P	P	P	P	P	P	P	P
16	F	F	F	F	F	F	F	F	F	F
17	P	P	P	P	P	P	P	P	P	P
18	P	P	P	P	P	P	P	P	P	P
19	P	P	P	P	P	P	P	P	P	P
20	F	P	P	P	P	P	P	P	P	P
21	P	F	F	F	F	F	F	F	F	F
22	P	P	P	P	P	P	P	P	P	P
23	P	P	P	P	P	P	P	P	P	P
24	P	P	P	P	P	P	P	P	P	P
25										

Then, we can proceed to do the analysis. The MINITAB path is: Stat>Quality Tools> Attribute Agreement Analysis. The results will look like this:

Attribute Agreement Analysis for Appraiser1 -, Appraiser1-2, Appraiser1-3, ...

Within Appraisers

```
Assessment Agreement

Appraiser  # Inspected  # Matched  Percent      95% CI
1              24           24      100.00  (88.27, 100.00)
2              24           23       95.83  (78.88,  99.89)
3              24           24      100.00  (88.27, 100.00)

# Matched: Appraiser agrees with him/herself across trials.
```

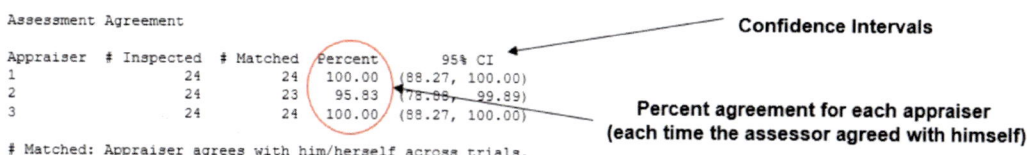

Confidence Intervals

Percent agreement for each appraiser
(each time the assessor agreed with himself)

Each Appraiser vs Standard

```
Assessment Agreement

Appraiser  # Inspected  # Matched  Percent      95% CI
1              24           22       91.67  (73.00, 98.97)
2              24           21       87.50  (67.64, 97.34)
3              24           22       91.67  (73.00, 98.97)

# Matched: Appraiser's assessment across trials agrees with the known standard.
```

Percent agreement for each appraiser
against the standard
(each time the assessor agreed with the standard)

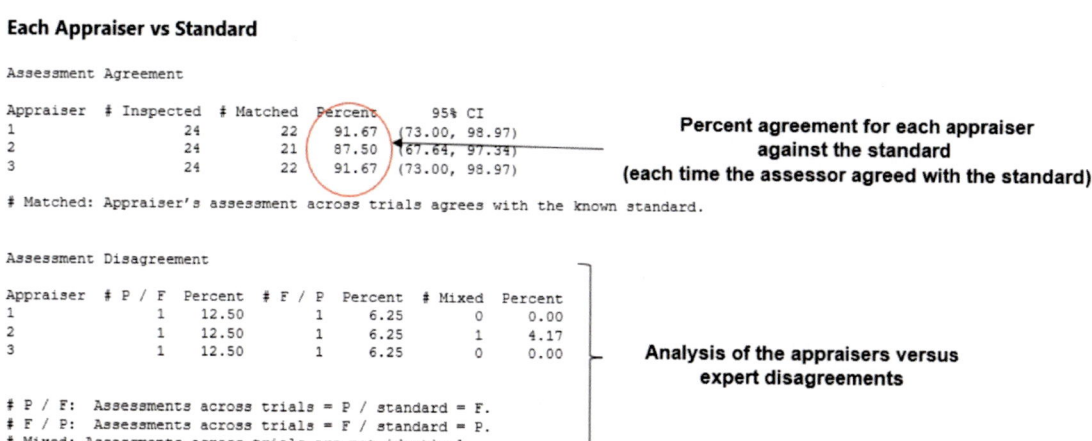

```
Assessment Disagreement

Appraiser  # P / F  Percent  # F / P  Percent  # Mixed  Percent
1            1       12.50      1      6.25       0      0.00
2            1       12.50      1      6.25       1      4.17
3            1       12.50      1      6.25       0      0.00

# P / F: Assessments across trials = P / standard = F.
# F / P: Assessments across trials = F / standard = P.
# Mixed: Assessments across trials are not identical.
```

Analysis of the appraisers versus expert disagreements

Between Appraisers

Assessment Agreement

```
# Inspected  # Matched  Percent      95% CI
    24          23       95.83   (78.88, 99.89)
```
Percent of the time the appraisers were in agreement with each other

Matched: All appraisers' assessments agree with each other.

All Appraisers vs Standard

Assessment Agreement

```
# Inspected  # Matched  Percent      95% CI
    24          21       87.50   (67.64, 97.34)
```
Agreement of all appraisers against the standard

Matched: All appraisers' assessments agree with the known standard.

Attribute Agreement Analysis

The graphical output for this analysis is very simple:

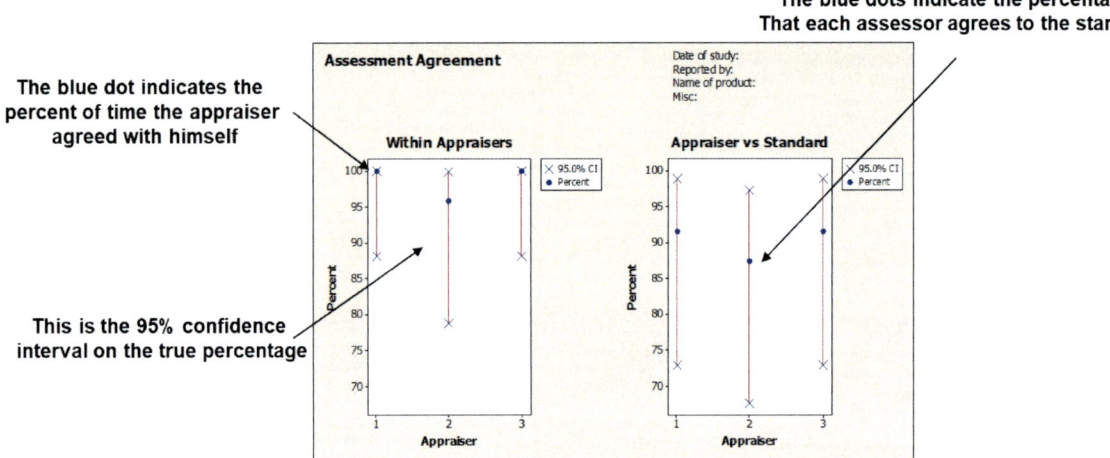

The blue dot indicates the percent of time the appraiser agreed with himself

This is the 95% confidence interval on the true percentage

The blue dots indicate the percentage That each assessor agrees to the standard

If the blue dots of one of the appraisers fall within the confidence interval of another appraiser, chances are that there is no statistical difference from the first appraiser to the second.

Usually every company establishes its own acceptance criteria for attribute R&R. Just as a recommendation, the typical criteria for acceptance of an attribute R&R is:

	Percent Agreement of all Appraisers Against the Standard
Good	90%-100%
Use with Caution	80%-90%
Unacceptable	<80%

45 | Page

Confidence Intervals

Definition

The degree of uncertainty when estimating a specific statistic value (point estimate) can be expressed as a confidence interval. For a fraction of a population we use what is called "tolerance interval".

When we refer to a 95% confidence interval for a point estimate, the industry will commonly interpret it as a 95% probability that the point estimate (i.e. the sample mean) will fall within the calculated confidence interval – which is a very practical interpretation. But a more accurate description would be (according to statisticians), that 95% of the intervals calculated from the samples would likely contain the true population point estimate, with a 5% probability that they would not.

Confidence intervals provide a range of values for a specific characteristic: the higher the confidence level, the more confident we are that the characteristic will fall within that range. The typical confidence levels are: 90%, 95%, and 99%.

Confidence Interval for the Mean

If we have a large enough sample with a normal distribution and a known standard deviation for the population, the calculation for the confidence interval for the mean is:

$$\bar{x} \pm Z_{\alpha/2} \; \sigma/\sqrt{n}$$

Where $\bar{x}$ is the sample mean, σ is the standard deviation of the population, and $Z_{\alpha/2}$ is the standardized value in the normal distribution for a given confidence level.

For small samples (based on the central limit theorem), the analysis is based on the T distribution and the formula is:

$$\bar{x} \pm t_{\alpha/2} \; S/\sqrt{n}$$

Where S is the standard deviation from the sample, and $t_{\alpha/2}$ has n-1 degrees of freedom – this value comes from a "T" statistical table.

To manually calculate this value ($Z_{\alpha/2}$, or $t_{\alpha/2}$) we would need statistical tables of the normal and T distribution. Fortunately, MINITAB provides that for us for almost every calculation (as we saw in previous chapters), for example, if we follow the MINITAB path: Stat>Basic Statistics>Graphical Summary, with a 95% confidence interval, we get:

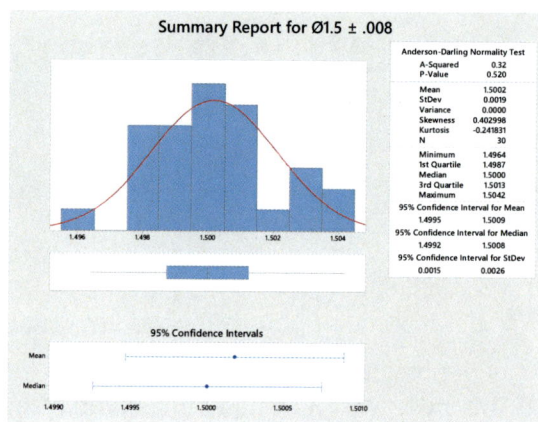

The confidence intervals for the mean, the median, and the standard deviation are automatically provided.

Following the same MINITAB path, if we change the confidence level to 99%, we get:

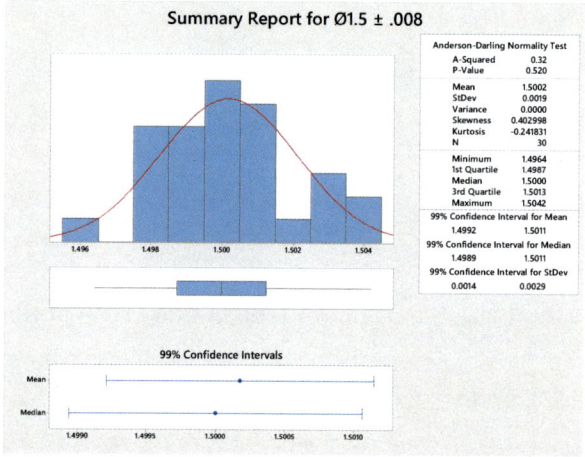

Notice how the range of the confidence intervals changed. In this case, the p value for normality is 0.520 and the sample can be considered normally distributed.

The confidence interval for the mean is also a good estimate for populations that are not normally distributed, but that is not the case for the confidence interval for the standard deviation.

Confidence Interval for the Variance

The confidence interval for the variance is not symmetrical from the point estimate. It is based on the Chi-square distribution. This is the formula:

$$\frac{(n-1) S^2}{\chi^2_{\alpha/2,\, n-1}} \leq \sigma^2 \leq \frac{(n-1) S^2}{\chi^2_{1-\alpha/2,\, n-1}}$$

The square root for each side of this equation will give us the confidence interval for the standard deviation. The condition of normality needs to be checked if we expect the analysis to be meaningful.

Confidence Intervals for Proportions (One sample)

Sometimes we may find it harder or we may encounter limitations when trying to collect variable data, and we can only get attribute data. If this is the case, the estimate of a confidence interval for a proportion (fraction nonconforming of attribute data) follows this formula:

$$p \pm Z_{\alpha/2} \sqrt{p(1-p)/n}$$

Where p is the sample proportion calculated by:

P = number of occurrences / Total sample size (n)

With the condition that: $np \geq 5$ and $n(1-p) \geq 5$

Example:

Let's assume that we randomly collected 80 samples from an assembly line, and 16 of them were defective, in order to know the 95% confidence interval for the proportion of defective parts we follow this MINITAB path: Stat>Basic Statistics>1 Proportion. Then select, "Summarized Data" in the drop-down menu and enter the data:

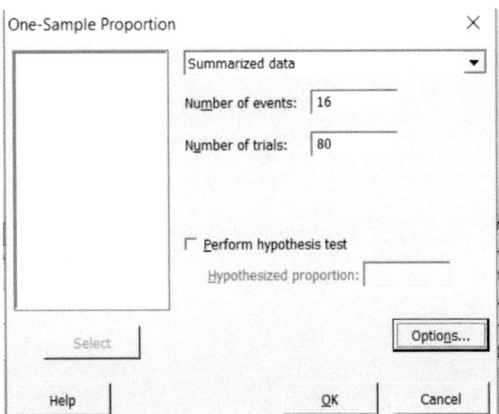

(Note that there is an option for hypothesis test, which we will not be performing yet. We will talk about that in the hypothesis test chapter of this handbook, page 54.)

This path allows for the confidence level value to be changed –if needed-- in "Options".

For our example above, the results will look like this:

Test and CI for One Proportion

```
Sample   X    N   Sample p          95% CI
1        16   80  0.200000   (0.118859, 0.304369)
```

Interpretation of the results: The 95% confidence interval for the proportion of defective parts will fall within a range of 11.886% and 30.437%

Confidence Interval for Proportions (2 samples)

Sometimes we need to calculate the confidence interval for the difference between two proportions from two different samples (including two different sample sizes). This is the formula:

$$p1 - p2 - Z_{\alpha/2} \sqrt{p1(1-p1)/n1 + p2(1-p2)/n2} \leq P1 - P2 \leq p1 - p2 + Z_{\alpha/2} \sqrt{p1(1-p1)/n1 + p2(1-p2)/n2}$$

Where pi is the sample proportion and ni is the sample size, i=1,2.

Following the last example, if we collect a second sample of 100 units and we get 15 defective ones, and thus enter the data into the path window as follows:

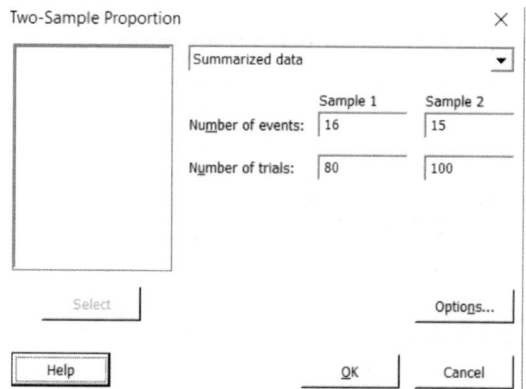

The results are:

Test and CI for Two Proportions

```
Sample   X    N    Sample p
1        16   80   0.200000
2        15   100  0.150000


Difference = p (1) - p (2)
Estimate for difference:  0.05
95% CI for difference:  (-0.0621641, 0.162164)
Test for difference = 0 (vs ≠ 0):  Z = 0.87   P-Value = 0.382

Fisher's exact test: P-Value = 0.429
```

Interpretation of the results: Both P-values are greater than 0.05, (in the hypothesis test chapter we will see how this means we failed to reject the null hypothesis), therefore the proportions from both samples are equal. Given that zero (0) falls within the confidence interval of (-0.0621641, 0.162164), we can claim consistency with the null hypothesis.

Confidence Interval for Defect Rates (One sample)

Sometimes we collect a sample and we count the number of defects per unit: Say we get 50 motorcycles from the assembly line and count the number of cosmetic defects per unit, which in this case add up to a total of 137 in all. If we want to calculate the confidence interval for the defect rate (10 or more units), we need to use the One-Sample Poisson test. This is the formula:

$$\bar{\lambda} - Z_{\alpha/2}\sqrt{\bar{\lambda}/n} \leq \lambda \leq \bar{\lambda} + Z_{\alpha/2}\sqrt{\bar{\lambda}/n}$$

Where $\bar{\lambda}$ is the sample defect rate

The MINITAB path is: Stat>Basic Statistics>1-Sample Poisson Rate

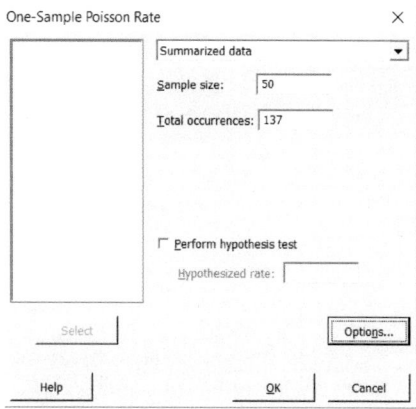

The results are:

Confidence Interval for One-Sample Poisson Rate

```
                Total           Rate of
Sample    Occurrences    N    Occurrence        95% CI
     1            137   50       2.74000   (2.30041, 3.23913)
```

"Length" of observation = 1.

Interpretation of the results: The rate of cosmetic defects per motorcycle is 2.74, and we are 95% confident that this rate will fall anywhere from 2.3 and 2.39 per unit.

Confidence Interval for Defect Rates (Two Samples)

The same principle from the 2-Sample proportion applies here for the 2-Sample defect rate. We want to know the confidence interval for the difference between a two-sample defect rate.

$$\bar{\lambda}_1 - \bar{\lambda}_2 - Z_{\alpha/2}\sqrt{\bar{\lambda}_1/n_1 - \bar{\lambda}_2/n_2} \leq \lambda_1 - \lambda_2 \leq \bar{\lambda}_1 - \bar{\lambda}_2 + Z_{\alpha/2}\sqrt{\bar{\lambda}_1/n_1 - \bar{\lambda}_2/n_2}$$

Expanding the last example, by taking a second sample of 40 motorcycles with a total of 80 defects in all, we have:

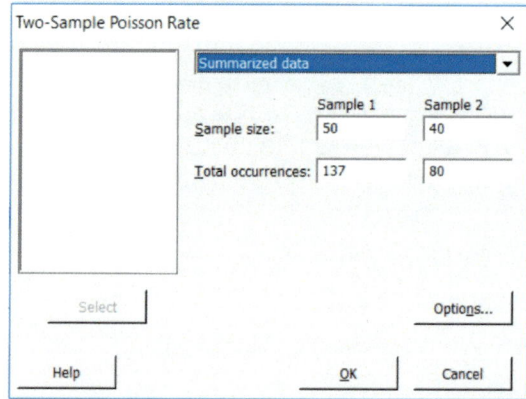

These are the results:

Test and CI for Two-Sample Poisson Rates

```
            Total        Rate of
Sample  Occurrences   N  Occurrence
1              137    50     2.74
2               80    40     2.00


Difference = rate(1) - rate(2)
Estimate for difference: 0.74
95% CI for difference: (0.105504, 1.37450)
Test for difference = 0 (vs ≠ 0): Z = 2.29 P-Value = 0.022

Exact Test: P-Value = 0.028
```

Interpretation of the results: The p value is under 0.05; hence we can clearly see that there is a statistical difference between both proportions. The confidence interval for the difference contains only positive numbers, so we can conclude with 95% confidence that the first sample has a higher defect rate than the second sample. As the Quality Engineer of this assembly line, I would start an investigation of the causes for the difference between defect rates.

Tolerance Intervals

Sometimes we need to know with a high degree of confidence what the lower and upper bounds are (statistical tolerance) for an individual characteristic of a given population. In order to calculate the tolerance interval, we first need to know the values of the confidence level, and the population fraction or proportion. We can calculate the tolerances with either variable or attribute data. On using this method, we rely on the assumption of normality for our data (if the data is not normally distributed we will have to use non-parametric methods or transform the data). We can calculate one sided or two-sided tolerance limits.

Example:

From a sample of 10 motorcycles, the horsepower in the dyno was recorded and we got an average of 75 horse-power maximum, with a standard deviation of 6.75. What is the 95% tolerance interval for the maximum horse-power for 80% of the production run?

The MINITAB path is: Stat>Quality Tools>Tolerance Interval then select once again "Summarize data". In the "Options" window select the Confidence level (95), the minimum percentage of the population interval (80), then select "Two-sided" - or if you want just one side select what side you are looking for.

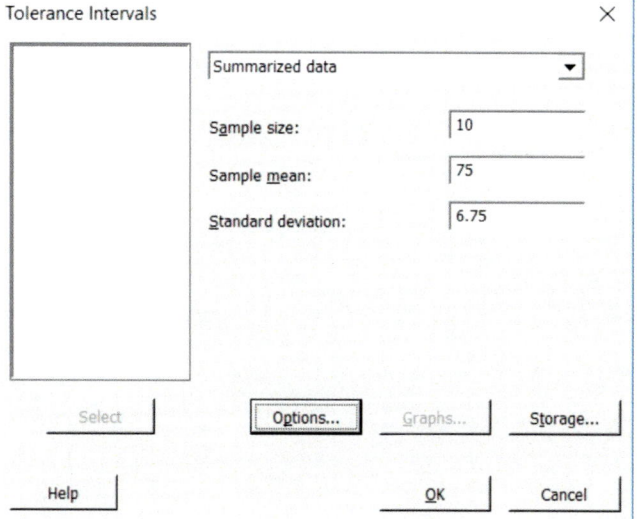

From the "Options" window:

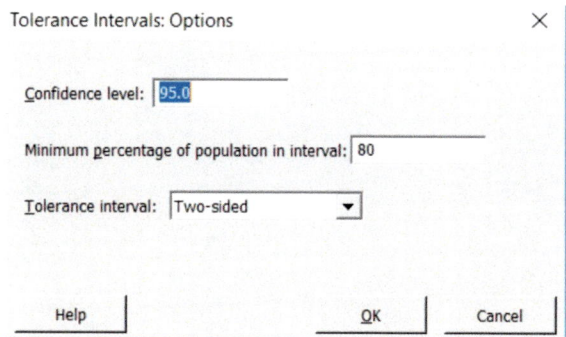

These are the results:

Tolerance Interval
```
Method
Confidence level                    95%
Percent of population in interval   80%

Statistics

 N    Mean    StDev
10   75.000   6.750

95% Tolerance Interval

                   Nonparametric     Achieved
   Normal Method       Method       Confidence
  (59.923, 90.077)  (x[1],  x[10])     62.4%

x[i] denotes the ith smallest observation.
```

Achieved confidence level applies only to nonparametric method

Interpretation of the results: The manufacturer can be 95% confident that 80% of the motorcycles will fall within 59.923 and 90.077 horsepower maximum range.

To calculate tolerance intervals for attribute data we need to go back to the one-sided confidence interval for proportion.

Hypothesis Test

Definition

The word "theory" is probably the most mis-used word in the world, a theory is a statement or idea that has already been proven true, while a hypothesis is a statement or idea that has not been proven true yet. In science and engineering many problems require for us to decide on whether to accept or reject a proposition on a specific parameter. This proposition is called "hypothesis", it is evaluated by comparison, and the process to prove or disprove the hypothesis is called "hypothesis test". Many problems in science and engineering can be formulated as hypothesis tests; and by using statistical tools we can make that decision on whether to reject or accept the hypothesis.

The initial baseline for the test is called the "Null hypothesis" (Ho) and assumes that there is no difference between the parameters/characteristics being compared. Examples are: no changes in process, no differences, or no relationships on parameters, etc.

The "alternative hypothesis" (Ha) is what we are attempting to test, and states there is a difference between the parameters or characteristics being compared. Examples are: different operating conditions, populations, or variations, etc.

Technically speaking, in a hypothesis test we don't "prove" the null hypothesis, we can either "fail to reject the null hypothesis" due to insufficient evidence, or "reject the null hypothesis" and accept the alternative hypothesis when there is enough evidence. This brings up the next 4 outcome possibilities for the hypothesis test:

	Accept Ho as True	Reject Ho as False
Ho is True	Correct Outcome (Confidence: 1-α)	Type I Error (α risk)
Ho is false	Type II Error (β risk)	Correct Outcome (Power: 1-β)

Type I Error (α Risk)

Type I error happens when we collect a random sample from the process which seems to contradict Ho, while Ho is actually true. The acceptable percentage of probability of occurrence for this error (called the alpha risk) needs to be defined before doing the study. Typically, a 5% (or 0.05) is selected. Therefore, 1-α is the confidence level of our test, it is the probability of rightfully accepting Ho – this is a good outcome!

For example: In previous chapters I mentioned the "p" value as a decision criterion for normality. It means, that if the p value is less than 0.05 (α risk), we reject Ho (the sample is normally distributed) and accept Ha (the sample is not normally distributed); and vice versa, if the p values is greater of 0.05, we fail to reject Ho of normality, and we can consider the sample normally distributed.

Type II Error (β Risk)

Type II error happens when we collect a random sample from the process that seems to support Ho while Ho is actually false. The probability of this error is called the beta risk, and it is typically set between 10% and 20%. Therefore, 1-β is the probability of correctly rejecting Ho and identifying Ha as true. This is the other good outcome of the test!

1-β is called "power", since this is the probability of rightfully rejecting Ho. We normally use a power of 80% or more.

Sequence for Hypothesis Testing

1. State the null hypothesis (Ho) and alternative hypothesis (Ha) --the wording will depend on the type of data and type of test we are performing
2. Establish α and β risk levels
3. Collect sample data
4. Perform the appropriate statistical tests, which will depend on the input and output variables.
5. Decide on whether or not to reject the Ho, based on p value.

Remember, we want α and β to be small, therefore the sample size needs to be calculated first, since p values are influenced by sample size. However, for a fixed sample size, we can't decrease one without increasing the other. For sample size determination calculations see the next chapter.

As an easy example of a hypothesis test we can use the case from the chapter on normal distribution, the normality test.

Ho: Sample approaches the normal distribution

Ha: Sample doesn't approach the normal distribution

We have a sample of 116 parts, after running the Anderson-Darling normality test with an α value of 0.05, we get:

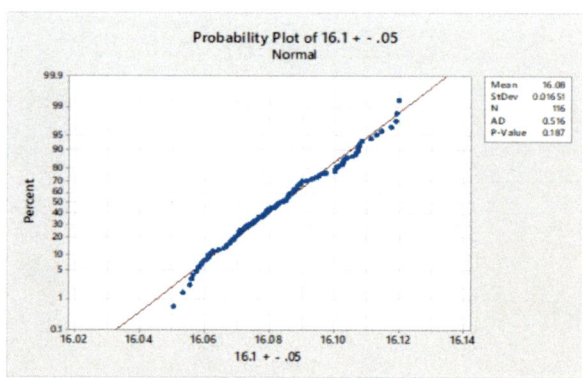

In this example the p value is 0.187, higher than 0.05, so we fail to reject the Ho, and assume that our sample approaches the normal distribution.

Hypothesis Test for One, Two, or More Samples

Usually we want to compare the parameters between samples. When this is the case, if we want to have a meaningful and reliable test, there are certain conditions that need to be met. For that, we need a roadmap, but before we see the roadmap one note: in this handbook we are only going to explain the most common tests that the quality and manufacturing engineer will have to deal with.

This is the roadmap:

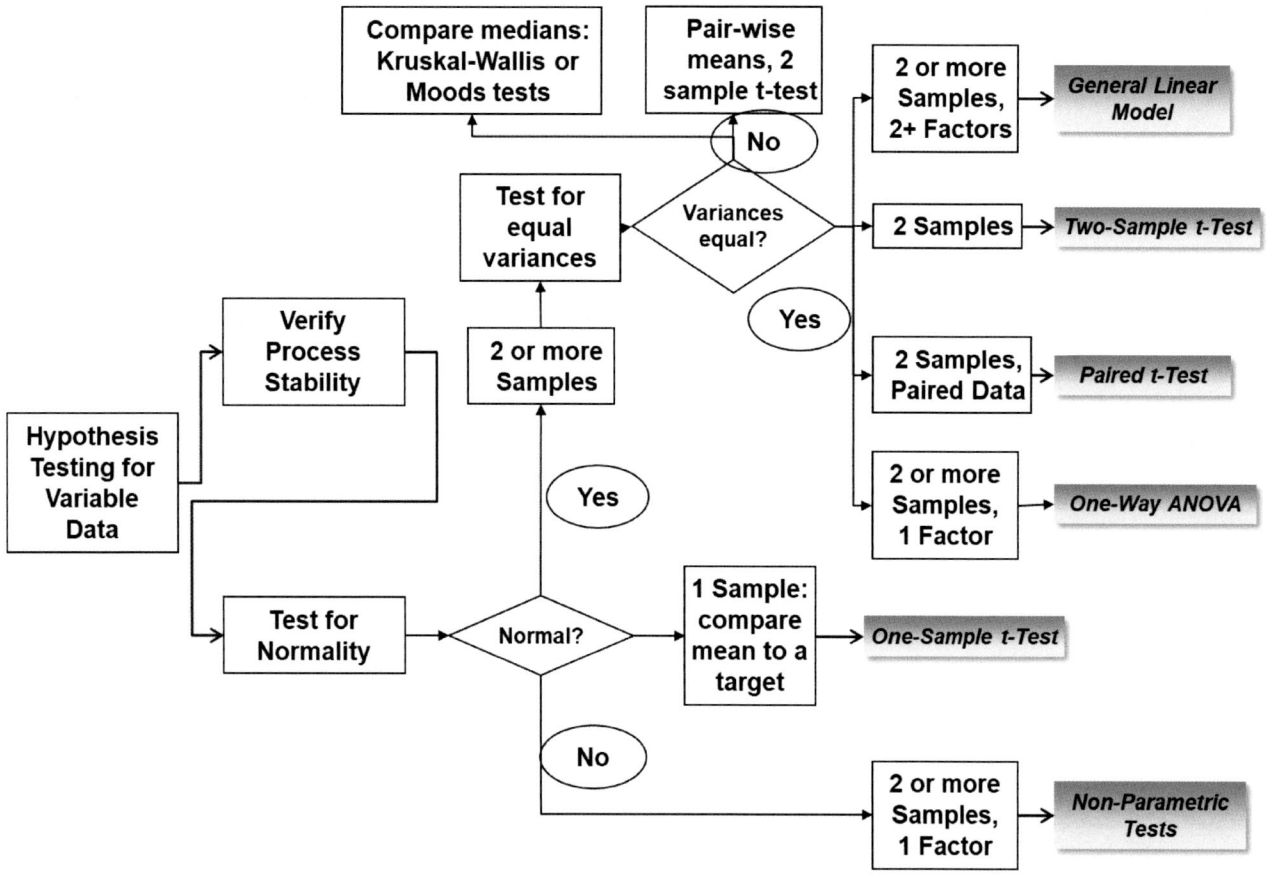

In previous chapters we explained how to test for stability (control charts), and normality (normality test). We are now going to focus on the remaining tests for samples:

Comparing One Mean to a Target:

To compare the mean of one single population to a target or known standard value, we perform a "one-sample t-test" – assuming we estimate σ from the sample. (If rather than estimating σ we know it directly from the actual population, then the formula changes to a Z-test.)

For this test, we can either have a one-sided test or a two-sided test:

Two-sided test.

Ho: μ = μo

Ha: μ ≠ μo

One sided test:

Ho: μ = μo

Ha: μ > μo

Or, μ < μo

Example:

Going back to the example of the motorcycles in a previous chapter, the sample size is 10, the average of the sample is 75 hp, and the standard deviation from the sample is 6.75 hp. The manufacturer advertises that the motorcycles have an average of 70 hp. Is there enough evidence to guarantee that all our motorcycles have 70 hp?

This is the hypothesis test:

Ho: µ = µo

Ha: µ ≠ µo

The path is: Stat>Basic Statistics>1-Sample T. In the dialog box we select "Summarized data":

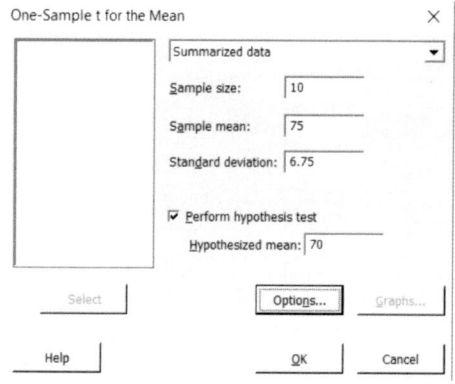

The result looks like this:

One-Sample T (Comparing sample mean to a target)

```
Test of µ = 70 vs ≠ 70


 N   Mean   StDev   SE Mean      95% CI          T      P
10  75.00    6.75      2.13   (70.17, 79.83)   2.34  0.044
```

Interpretation of the results: Since the P value is less than 0.05 the null hypothesis is rejected, the average of the sample is statistically significantly higher than 70 hp (look at the 95% confidence interval), to the benefit of the manufacturer.

Test for Equal Variances

To have a meaningful comparison of means between 2 or more populations, they must be within the same process variability, so the variances need to be compared and tested. The test we will use for that is the F-test (review chapter on distribution if needed).

The hypothesis test looks like this:

Ho: $\sigma^2_A = \sigma^2_B$

Ha: $\sigma^2_A \neq \sigma^2_B$

Example:

We want to analyze the speed variation in two different conveyors, in ft/minute. We collect 10 different speeds, 5 for each line, and we get this data:

Speed	Assy. Line
10.1	A
10.0	A
9.8	A
10.5	A
9.7	A
10.2	B
10.4	B
10.0	B
9.9	B
10.1	B

To test for equal variances the path is: Stat>ANOVA>Test for equal variances.

The results are:

Test for Equal Variances: Speed versus Assy. Line
Method

```
Null hypothesis         All variances are equal
Alternative hypothesis  At least one variance is different
Significance level      α = 0.05

95% Bonferroni Confidence Intervals for Standard Deviations

Assy.
 Line  N    StDev           CI
   A   5  0.311448   (0.107722, 1.63210)
   B   5  0.192354   (0.071822, 0.93374)

Individual confidence level = 97.5%

Tests
                        Test
Method               Statistic   P-Value
Multiple comparisons    0.84      0.358
Levene                  0.64      0.447
```

The P-value is higher than 0.05, therefore, we fail to reject the null hypothesis and we can consider the speed variation from both conveyors to be equal. However, with only 5 observations on each group, we should consider collecting more data to increase the power of the test.
Graphical Output:

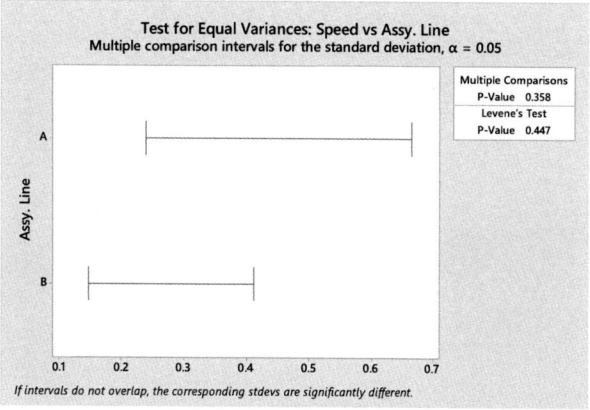

Analysis of Variance (ANOVA) - Means

This test helps to determine if the means of two or more groups are different from each other, assuming variances do not differ statistically from each other across the groups.

Don't let the name confuse you (ANOVA), this test is not comparing the variances per se, but rather allowing the comparison of the means by breaks down the variation into its components including the error or process noise.

Example:

Adding a third group of data to the last example, the path is: Stat>ANOVA>One way. The results are:

One-way ANOVA: Speed versus Assy. Line
```
Method

Null hypothesis:         All means are equal
Alternative hypothesis:  At least one mean is different
Significance level       α = 0.05

Equal variances were assumed for the analysis.

Factor Information

Factor        Levels  Values
Assy. Line         3  A, B, C

Analysis of Variance

Source      DF  Adj SS   Adj MS  F-Value  P-Value
Assy. Line   2   1.033  0.51667     5.94    0.016
Error       12   1.044  0.08700
Total       14   2.077

Model Summary
        S    R-sq  R-sq(adj)  R-sq(pred)
 0.294958  49.74%     41.37%      21.47%

Means

Assy.
Line   N     Mean   StDev        95% CI
A      5   10.020   0.311  ( 9.733,  10.307)
B      5  10.1200  0.1924  (9.8326, 10.4074)
C      5    9.520   0.356  ( 9.233,   9.807)

Pooled StDev = 0.294958
```

> The different factor levels only explain 41.37% of the variability

The P value is under 0.05, which means that at least one mean is statistically different from at least another one. This is the graphical outcome:

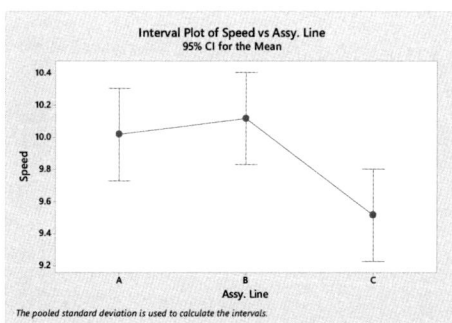

The confidence intervals from conveyor B and C do not overlap, which indicate a significant difference. This analysis and the graphical outcome also provide some analysis of residuals:

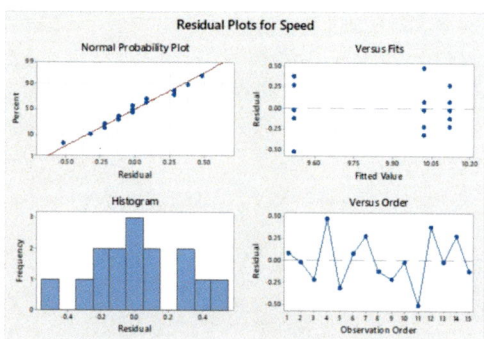

Residuals should be in control

Residuals should also be normally distributed. If patterns are shown in the charts it means that the model is not explaining the data –there is something wrong with either the sample or the process.

Comparing Two Independent Samples – Analysis of Means

This test is basically designed to compare the means of two samples to prove whether or not they have a common population mean, assuming unknown standard deviations from the populations. The samples are considered independent because the results of one group have no impact on the results of the other group.

This is the hypothesis test:

Ho: $\mu_1 = \mu_2$

Ha: $\mu_1 \neq \mu_2$

Sometimes the hypothesis test is expressed:

Ho: $\mu_1 - \mu_2 = 0$

Ha: $\mu_1 - \mu_2 \neq 0$

Example:

Say we machine the same characteristic of a metallic component in two different lathes, and take 2 different size samples. Then we follow the path: Stat>Basic Statistics>2-Sample t. This is the result:

Two-Sample T-Test and CI: Ø 1 ± .02 (1 of 2)_4, Ø 1 ± .02 (2 of 2)_3

```
Two-sample T for Ø 1 ± .02 (1 of 2)_4 vs Ø 1 ± .02 (2 of 2)_3

                      N     Mean    StDev   SE Mean
Ø 1 ± .02 (1 of 2)_4  46   0.99714  0.00306  0.00045
Ø 1 ± .02 (2 of 2)_3  30   0.98891  0.00239  0.00044


Difference = μ (Ø 1 ± .02 (1 of 2)_4) - μ (Ø 1 ± .02 (2 of 2)_3)
Estimate for difference:  0.008232
95% CI for difference:    (0.006914, 0.009551)
```

```
T-Test of difference = 0 (vs ≠): T-Value = 12.44   P-Value = 0.000   DF = 74
Both use Pooled StDev = 0.0028
```

The P value is under 0.05, therefore, we reject the null hypothesis of no difference in the means, and we conclude that there is a statistically significant difference between the means from both samples. In the example below the measurements are in millimeters. Look how close the means and the standard deviations are from each other, and yet, they are statistically different. This is the graphical outcome:

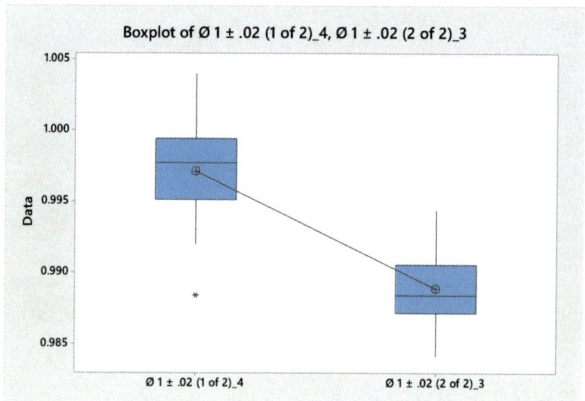

Practical Significance versus Statistical Significance

This is a good moment to mention that not every statistical difference means there is a practical difference. Based on the last example, given the measurements are in millimeters, the difference between both sample means is just 0.00823mm, and the difference in the sample standard deviations is just 0.00067mm. Now, let's plot both samples against wider specification limits:

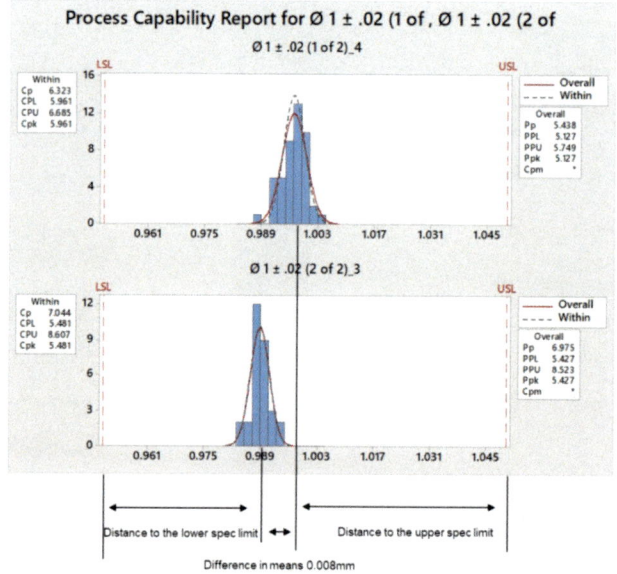

The process is centered and normally distributed. If the specification limits are ±0.05mm, then our production is far enough from the limits (very high Cpk and Ppk for both samples) to where there is no significant difference between both samples, practically speaking. Assuming this feature is for a noncritical or low critical characteristic (based on the design risk analysis), we can say that the difference between both samples is not practically significant.

Paired T-Test

When we have two samples and one of them can be classified as "before" a change, and the second sample classified as "after" a change or improvement, we use the paired t-test, (both samples must be the same size).

Example:

Going back to the last example, let's assume that after machining those two samples we submit the parts of one of them to anodization. We measure the same characteristic again. Then, after performing a paired t-test, the results are:

The hypothesis test is:

Ho: µ1 = µ2

Ha: µ1 ≠ µ2

Paired T-Test and CI: Ø 1 ± .02 (1 of 2)_4, Ø 1 ± .02 (2 of 2)_4

```
Paired T for Ø 1 ± .02 (1 of 2)_4 - Ø 1 ± .02 (2 of 2)_4

                       N      Mean     StDev   SE Mean
Ø 1 ± .02 (1 of 2)_4  46  0.997139  0.003065  0.000452
Ø 1 ± .02 (2 of 2)_4  46  0.996857  0.003162  0.000466
Difference            46  0.000283  0.002755  0.000406


95% CI for mean difference: (-0.000536, 0.001101)
T-Test of mean difference = 0 (vs ≠ 0): T-Value = 0.70  P-Value = 0.490
```

The P value is above 0.05, therefore, we failed to reject the null hypothesis and we assume that there is no statistical difference for this characteristic before and after anodization.

Comparing Multiple Nested Samples (Means) – ANOVA

We already explained the process to compare multiple means, but when the samples collected come from specific levels, hierarchies, or subgroups within subgroups, we must use the nested method. In other words, if we collect samples from multiple production lots, from different assembly lines, and from different factories, then we use the nested method. In this method we can have a different number of responses and a different number of factors. Here we also assume normality and equal variances.

If the sampling method is not hierarchical and we have a fixed factor, then we use the Balanced ANOVA or the General Linear Model (this method is not covered in this handbook).

Example:

We receive the same product from 4 different machines, then we segregate two production lots from each machine, finally we measure one characteristic from 2 parts from each of the lots. The results are:

Machine A	Lot 1	9.902	9.900
	Lot 2	9.896	9.930
Machine B	Lot 1	9.914	9.898
	Lot 2	9.900	9.906
Machine C	Lot 1	9.960	0.008
	Lot 2	10.004	9.986
Machine D	Lot 1	9.940	0.032
	Lot 2	10.064	9.958

The null hypothesis is that the means of all machines are the same while the alternative hypothesis is that at least one mean is different from the rest. The path is: Stat>ANOVA>Fully Nested ANOVA.

The results are:

Nested ANOVA: Measurement versus Lot No., Machine No.

```
Analysis of Variance for Measurement

Source        DF      SS        MS        F       P
Lot No.        1   0.0005    0.0005    0.075   0.794
Machine No.    6   0.0406    0.0068   17.731   0.000
Error          8   0.0031    0.0004
Total         15   0.0441

Variance Components
                           % of
Source        Var Comp.   Total   StDev
Lot No.        -0.001*     0.00   0.000
Machine No.     0.003     89.32   0.056
Error           0.000     10.68   0.020
Total           0.004             0.060

* Value is negative, and is estimated by zero.

Expected Mean Squares

1  Lot No.        1.00(3) + 2.00(2) + 8.00(1)
2  Machine No.    1.00(3) + 2.00(2)
3  Error          1.00(3)
```

Interpretation of the results: The P values show that there is not enough evidence to reject the null hypothesis for lot number, but there is a statistically significant difference by machine number. We can conclude that the production lots by machine are consistent but there is a difference between machines.

We also get the "Variance Components", from the % column, and conclude that 89% of the variation is caused by the machine and 10.6% by the error.

Test for Proportions

In the previous roadmap we didn't mention the hypothesis tests available for attribute data (that would require a different roadmap). Here we are only going to explain two of them: comparing one sample to target value/standard and comparing two independent samples for a one (or two if required) tailed test.

Comparing One Proportion to a Standard

We can compare a proportion to a target value or standard using a Z-test, following the normal distribution. For the hypothesis test P1 is the sample proportion and Po is the standard or target value.

Ho: $P_1 = P_o$

Ha: $P_1 \neq P_o$

The path is: Stat>Basic Statistics>1 Proportion

Example:

We collect a sample of 100 air conditioners, 10 of them show leaks, but marketing reports that only 1% have leaks on the field. Is there enough evidence to suggest that the actual leak rate is different from 1%?

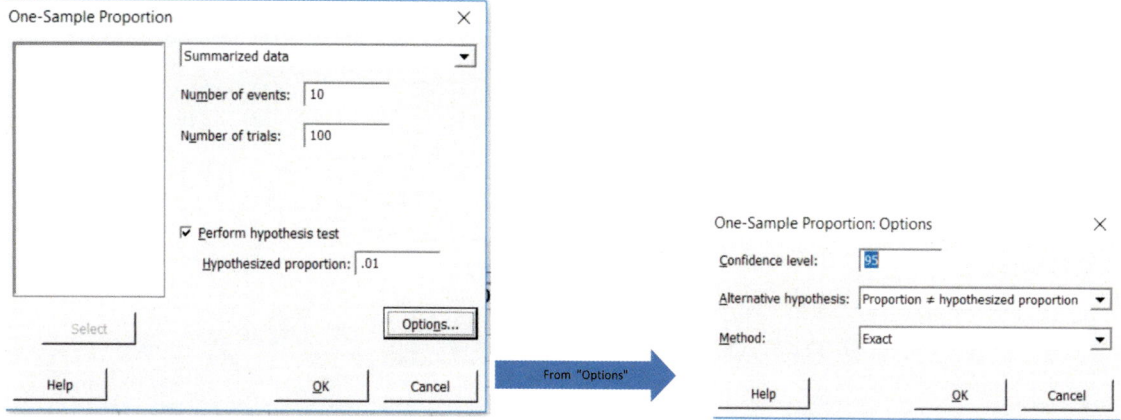

These are the results:

Test and CI for One Proportion

```
Test of p = 0.01 vs p ≠ 0.01

                                          Exact
Sample   X    N   Sample p      95% CI      P-Value
1       10   100  0.100000  (0.049005, 0.176223)  0.000
```

There is enough evidence to reject the null hypothesis that the leak rate is 1%.

Comparing two Independent Proportions

Comparing two independent proportions (for multiple independent proportions we would use a chi-square test) usually follows the Z-test as well. However, for small sample sizes or extreme proportions an F-test is required instead.

For the hypothesis test P1 is the sample 1 proportion and P2 is the proportion of the second sample.

Ho: $P_1 = P_2$

Ha: $P_1 \neq P_2$

The path is: Stat>Basic Statistics>2 Proportion

Example:

From the previous case, let's now compare the proportion of leakage to a similar sample from another factory where we found 5 leaking units. The results are:

Test and CI for Two Proportions

```
Sample    X     N    Sample p
1         10    100  0.100000
2         5     100  0.050000

Difference = p (1) - p (2)
Estimate for difference:  0.05
95% CI for difference:  (-0.0226774, 0.122677)
Test for difference = 0 (vs ≠ 0):  Z = 1.35   P-Value = 0.178

Fisher's exact test: P-Value = 0.283
```

Based on the P value, there is not enough evidence to reject the null hypothesis and we can consider both proportions similar.

The nice thing about this test is that we can have different sample sizes and we can also perform this test to a hypothesized difference (P1 – P2 ≠ 0).

Power of Comparing Two Proportions

We already explained how to compare proportions. In this chapter we also explained the "power" (probability to reject Ho when Ho is actually false, 1-β) of a test. When we test two proportions, it is useful to calculate the power of our test. This is related to our sample size. The purpose of estimating the power of our test is to find out if it is high enough to detect the difference between both proportions.

Calculating this can be tricky, because we need to define how much difference we want to detect before actually conducting the test.

Take the last example: we would want to estimate the power if we aim to detect a difference of either 50% (0.5) or 10% (0.1).

The results are:

Power and Sample Size

```
Test for Two Proportions

Testing comparison p = baseline p (versus ≠)
Calculating power for baseline p = 0.1
α = 0.05

                Sample
Comparison p    Size     Power
        0.5     100      1.00000

The sample size is for each group.
```

Interpretation: Power is 1.0, therefore, for two sample sizes of 100, there is a 100% power detecting a 50% difference in proportions.

Now, to detect a 10% difference:

Power and Sample Size

```
Test for Two Proportions

Testing comparison p = baseline p (versus ≠)
Calculating power for baseline p = 0.1
α = 0.05

              Sample
Comparison p   Size     Power
      0.01     100    0.801831

The sample size is for each group.
```

Interpretation: Power is 0.801, therefore, for two sample sizes of 100, there is an 80% power detecting a 10% difference in proportions.

Power Curve for Two Proportions
We also get a graphical output. It represents every combination of power and comparison values for a sample size of 100.

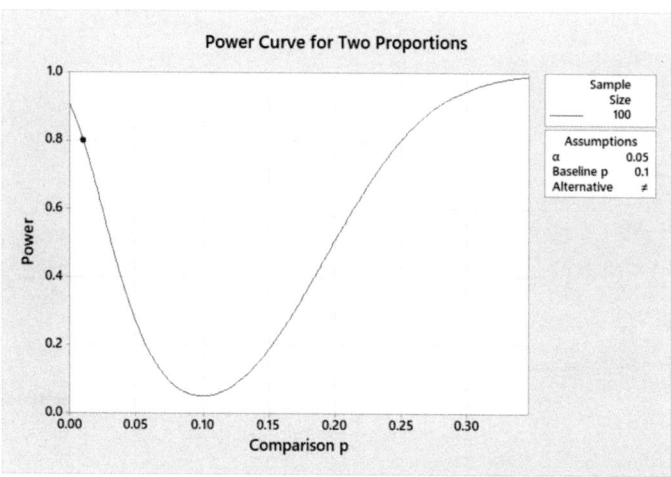

Sample Size Determination

Ideally, we would like to measure 100% of a given population, but it is hardly feasible due to time, cost, and space limitations. Even if we could do it, the measurement error would prevent us from knowing the true values. But we can still use samples to estimate an acceptable approximation to the true values of a population.

There are some basic requirements for sampling: the samples must be random and independent.

There are different sampling designs that can be used depending on the project:

- Simple random sampling
- Systematic sampling
- Subgroups, stratified, hierarchical, block, and clustered sampling among others.

The sampling design that we will use will also depend on the hypothesis that we want to test.

Sample Size Calculation with Known Standard Deviation (σ) and Normal Distribution

This is probably the easiest way to calculate the sample size to detect margin of error of a parameter. For this estimate we only need to know the standard deviation and the difference (margin of error) that we aim to detect.

For Example:

We know that the σ of a process is 20, and we aim to detect a difference on the mean (parameter) of 2. The path is: Stat>Power and Sample Size>n Sample Size for Estimation.

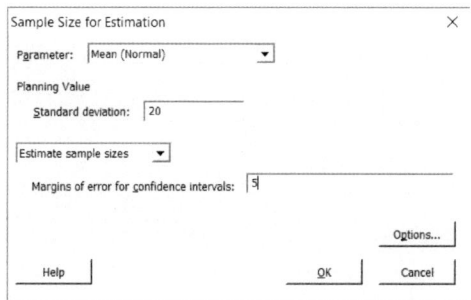

The results are:

Sample Size for Estimation

```
Method

Parameter           Mean
Distribution        Normal
Standard deviation  20 (estimate)
Confidence level    95%
Confidence interval Two-sided

Results
```

```
 Margin   Sample
of Error   Size
     5      64
```

The results show that we need 64 samples to detect this margin of error in the means. This method can also help us to calculate other parameters, such as standard deviation, proportions, variance, rates and means (Poisson).

Variable Data, 1 Sample Z

To calculate the sample size to estimate a mean at a certain confidence level and a known standard deviation (σ), we use a Z distribution estimate. It requires 2 known variables: the standard deviation of the population, and the difference that we aim to detect between the means. We also need to define the α and 1-β levels of our test.

Example:

If we know that the standard deviation of one product characteristic coming out of our process is 0.05mm, and we want to take a sample to detect a change in means that up to 0.02mm with a 95% confidence and a power of 95%. We follow the path: Stat>Power and Sample Size>1-Sample Z.

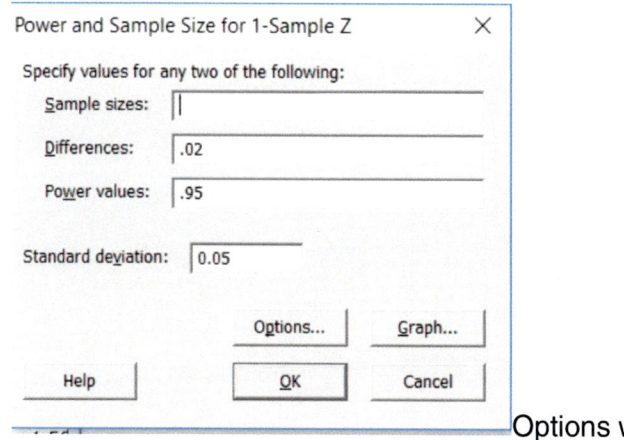

Options window: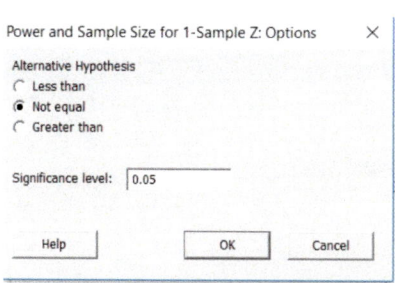

Power and Sample Size

```
1-Sample Z Test

Testing mean = null (versus ≠ null)
Calculating power for mean = null + difference
α = 0.05   Assumed standard deviation = 0.05

            Sample   Target
Difference   Size    Power    Actual Power
    0.02      82      0.95       0.951763
```

Power Curve for 1-Sample Z Test

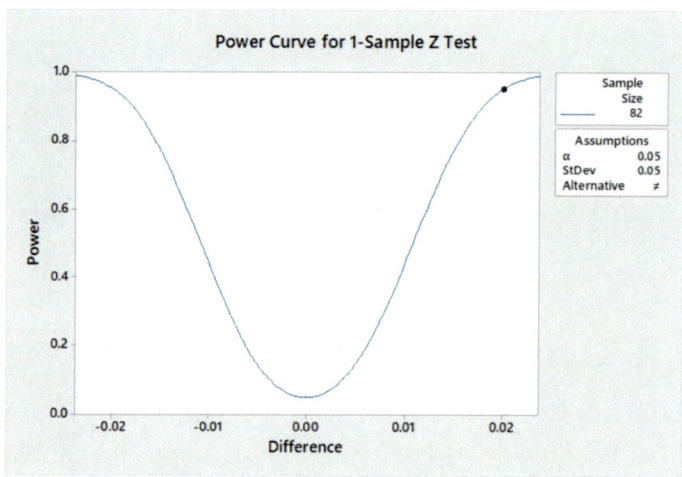

In this example we need 82 samples to detect a difference of 0.02mm in our process.

Variable Data, 1 Sample T

To calculate the sample size to estimate a mean at a certain confidence level and a given standard deviation from the sample (s), we use a T-test estimate. Note: for this calculation the standard deviation comes from the sample, not the population. This test requires 2 known variables: the standard deviation of the samples and the difference that we aim to detect between the means. We also need to define the α and 1-β levels of our test.

Using the same data from the previous example, assuming the sample standard deviation is 0.05mm. with a 95% confidence and a power of 95%. We follow the path: Stat>Power and Sample Size>1-Sample t. The results are:

Power and Sample Size

```
1-Sample t Test

Testing mean = null (versus ≠ null)
Calculating power for mean = null + difference
α = 0.05  Assumed standard deviation = 0.06

            Sample  Target
Difference    Size   Power  Actual Power
     0.024      84    0.95      0.951879
```

Therefore, we would need 84 samples to estimate a difference of 0.024mm with 95% confidence and 95% power.

Variable Data, 2 Sample Paired T

To calculate the sample size to estimate the difference between to sample means at a certain confidence level and a given standard deviation from the sample (s), we use a 2 Sample T-test estimate. Note: for this calculation the standard deviation comes from the sample, not the population. This test requires 2 known variables: the standard deviation from the samples and the difference that we aim to detect between the means. We also need to define the α and 1-β levels of our test.

Using the same data from the previous example, assuming the pooled sample standard deviation is 0.06mm, and we aim to detect a difference of 0.05mm with a 95% confidence and a power of 95%. We follow the path: Stat>Power and Sample Size>Paired t.

The results are:

```
Paired t Test

Testing mean paired difference = 0 (versus ≠ 0)
Calculating power for mean paired difference = difference
α = 0.05  Assumed standard deviation of paired differences = 0.06

            Sample  Target
Difference   Size   Power   Actual Power
   0.05       21     0.95      0.952524
```

Then we need a sample size of 21 to detect a difference of 0.05mm between sample means, with a 95% confidence and 95% power.

Variable Data, 2 Sample T-Test

To calculate the sample size when the standard deviation (σ) comes from the population (not the samples), we use a 2 Sample T-Test. This test requires 2 known variables: the standard deviation of the population and the difference that we aim to detect between the means. We also need to define the α and 1-β levels of our test.

Using the same data from our last example, but now calculating for two different powers (80% and 95%). We follow the path: Stat>Power and Sample Size>2-Sample t.

The results are:

Power and Sample Size
```
2-Sample t Test

Testing mean 1 = mean 2 (versus ≠)
Calculating power for mean 1 = mean 2 + difference
α = 0.05  Assumed standard deviation = 0.06

            Sample  Target
Difference   Size   Power   Actual Power
   0.05       39     0.95      0.952841
   0.05       24     0.80      0.806767

The sample size is for each group.
```

> Notice how the sample size, changes according to the change on power (1-β) levels.

Sample Size for Attribute Data – Binomial Distribution

The binomial event occurs when there are two possible outcomes from the assessment, good vs bad. There are two ways to calculate the sample size for binomial hypothesis.

1. Using the α and β levels, and a comparison proportion
2. Calculating the confidence interval and comparing it to a lower and upper bound

For the first method, as stated above, we use the values for the α and β levels, and a comparison proportion, and then follow the same process described previously in this chapter. The path is:

Stat>Power and Sample Size>1 Proportion. In this option we enter any two of these values and the software will calculate the third one.

```
Power and Sample Size for 1 Proportion                    X

Specify values for any two of the following:
    Sample sizes:            [            ]
    Comparison proportions:  [            ]
    Power values:            [            ]

    Hypothesized proportion: [            ]

                                    Options...    Graph...
    Help                            OK            Cancel
```

This first method can be confusing because the comparison proportion refers to the difference between the two hypothesized proportions.

The second method is very straight forward, it is done by simply calculating the confidence level for the proportion. We don't even need the value for the β level. We can create our own table of sample sizes after the iteration of different values. The iteration will be determined by the maximum number of failures from the several trials still rendering an acceptable test result (within a predetermined p value) – assuming a constant confidence level (which can be changed from one test to the next). For this method we need to pre-determine a reliability level –desired proportion of successes in our population. Having done that, we can start iterating variables.

For example: Let's assume that we want to conduct an experiment where we aim to guarantee that more than 90% of the customers will get a benefit from our product (we will call this value reliability). We want to have a 95% confidence, and zero failures in our test.

This is the hypothesis test:

Ho: P1 = 0.90

Ha: P1 > 0.90

The path is: Stat>Basic Statistics>1 Proportion.

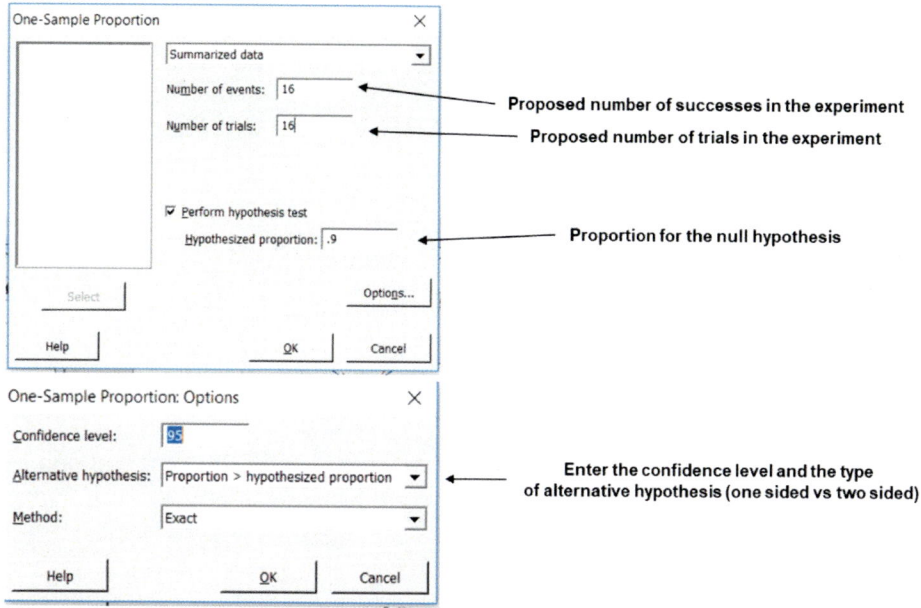

Test and CI for One Proportion

```
Test of p = 0.9 vs p > 0.9
                                        Exact
Sample   X    N   Sample p   95% Lower Bound   P-Value
1        16   16  1.000000           0.829250    0.185
```

Results: The lower bound is 82.9% which is under the 90% pre-determined reliability for the experiment. The p value is above 0.05 so we can't reject the null hypothesis and we can't guarantee that more than 90% of the customers will get a benefit from our product from testing just 16 parts.
Look what happens when we re-run the experiment and use a sample size of 29, under the same confidence and reliability levels and zero failures.

Test and CI for One Proportion

```
Test of p = 0.9 vs p > 0.9
                                        Exact
Sample   X    N   Sample p   95% Lower Bound   P-Value
1        29   29  1.000000           0.901855    0.047
```

In this result the lower bound is just above 90% and the p value is under 0.05, we can reject the null hypothesis and conclude that if we test 29 parts and none of them fail, we can say that our product will benefit more than 90% percent of the customers.
If we re-run the experiment with the same data, but we allow 1 failure out of 29 parts in our test the results are:

Test and CI for One Proportion

```
Test of p = 0.9 vs p > 0.9
                                        Exact
Sample   X    N   Sample p   95% Lower Bound   P-Value
1        28   29  0.965517           0.846608    0.199
```

Allowing 1 failure out of 29 parts in our test will mean that we failed to reject the null hypothesis. Let's do this one more time with 46 samples and 1 failure, the results are:

Test and CI for One Proportion

```
Test of p = 0.9 vs p > 0.9
                                              Exact
Sample   X    N   Sample p   95% Lower Bound  P-Value
1        45   46  0.978261          0.900976  0.048
```

Using the same methodology, we would have to move our sample size up to 46 in order to pass the test while allowing 1 failure.

It is always convenient to create a table with the multiple combinations of the different conditions for our test. This is an example of a table showing the sample size for a hypothesis test where:
Ho: P1 = 0.60

Ha: P1 > 0.60

With 95% confidence level, 60% reliability, and allowing 1 or 2 failures (maximum failures allowed for this test to pass).

Hypothesis Testing Table - Population Proportion ρ, using a Binomial Distribution				
Trials	No. of Successes	Probability of Success	95% Lower Bound	p-value < 0.05
10	9	90%	60.58%	0.046
11	10	81%	63.50%	0.03
12	11	91%	66.00%	0.019
13	12	92%	68.30%	0.013
14	12	86%	61.40%	0.04

If we don't allow any failures during the test, our table changes and it will look like this:

Hypothesis Testing Table - Population Proportion ρ, using a Binomial Distribution				
Trials	No. of Successes	Probability of Success	95% Lower Bound	p-value < 0.05
8	8	100%	68.76%	0.017
9	9	100%	71.68%	0.01
10	10	100%	74.11%	0.006
11	11	100%	76.16%	0.004
12	12	100%	77.90%	0.002
13	13	100%	79.42%	0.001
14	14	100%	80.74%	0.001

Regression Analysis

Linear regression is very useful to create a mathematical model for a cause-effect relationship between two variables: an input (predictor) and a response variable. In other words, the value of one variable can be predicted from that of another variable.

When having two variables, we can make a distinction between a functional relation from a statistical relation. A functional relation is defined by an equation in the form of:

$$Y = f(X)$$

A statistical relation is established by statistical analysis, where not all the points will fall into the model. This is more like a probabilistic relation. Before we go directly into this topic we need to establish some basic concepts.

Correlation Coefficient (r)

The correlation coefficient is usually indicated by "r" and measures the strength of the linear relationship between two variables: one dependent variable Y and one independent variable X. This coefficient comes directly from the coefficient of determination (r^2) defined as:

$$0 \leq r^2 \leq 1$$

This (r^2) is the measure of the proportionate reduction of total variation associated with the use of the independent variable X. Thus, the larger r^2, the more is the total variation of Y.

Therefore, the correlation coefficient (r) is defined by: $\pm \sqrt{r^2}$

Then the range of r is: $-1 \leq r \leq 1$. This number it the most used in determining correlation between two variables. If r has a negative value it indicates a negative correlation or negative slope, while if r has a positive value, it indicates a positive correlation or positive slope in the curve. The larger the value of r, the stronger the correlation. If r is zero, it means that there is no linear correlation between the variables.

The coefficient of determination can measure the proportion of variation in Y that is caused/explained by X, and it is usually expressed in percentages.

Simple Linear and Non-Linear Regression

Simple linear regression applies for variable Y, and X data; and we aim to understand the relationship between two variables by creating a mathematical model (equation). The basic mathematical model is:

$$Y = \beta_0 + \beta_1 X_1$$

Where β_0 is the constant and β_1 is the coefficient for X_1. β_0 is defined as the intercept value (where the line crosses the Y axis, and β_1 as the slope (rise over run) value.

Using the least squares method, computers can make the analysis for us – unless you want to do it by hand using linear algebra. The computer will calculate the fit line (prediction equation –see below) to the data:

These are graphic examples of positive, negative, and no linear correlation between variables:

The red line is the mathematical model and is called the "fitted line", "prediction equation", or "fits".

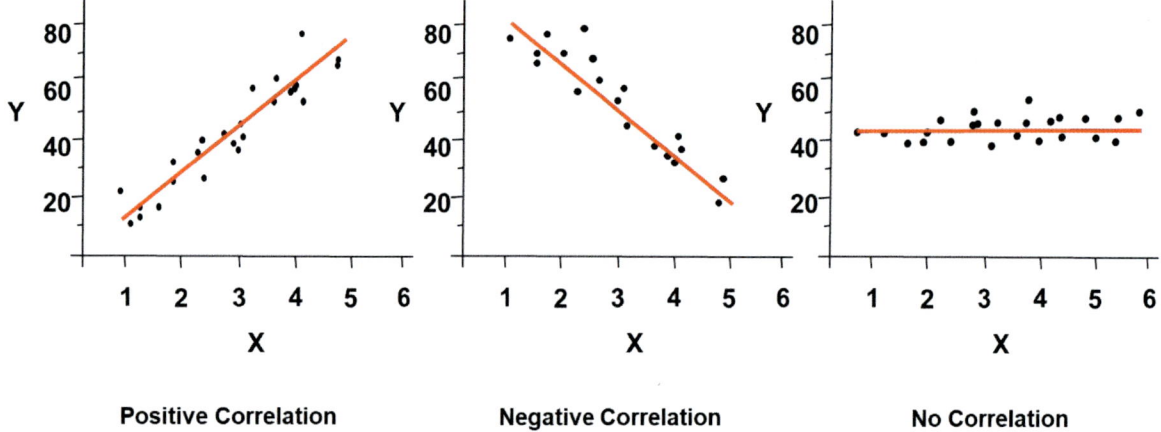

Positive Correlation   Negative Correlation   No Correlation

Not all the points in our data will fit the equation. The distance between the points and the estimated line or predicted value is called "residual".

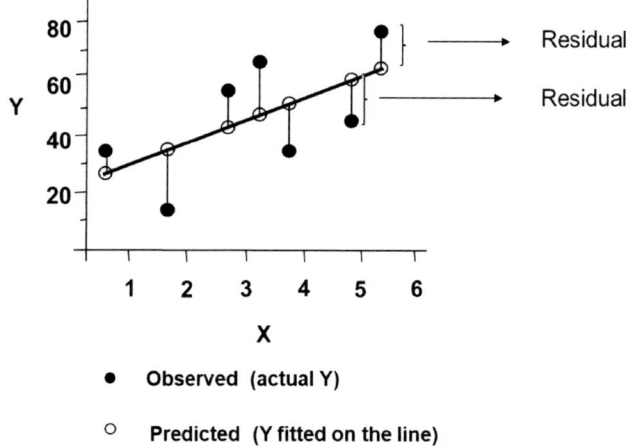

●   Observed (actual Y)

○   Predicted (Y fitted on the line)

Before we jump into an example, we need to create a roadmap that will help us follow the regression analysis steps in the proper order:

```
┌─────────────────────────────────────────────────────────────┐
│ Plan the study and identify the 2 variables in term of cause and effect │
└─────────────────────────────────────────────────────────────┘
                              │
                              ▼
              ┌──────────────────────────────────┐
              │ Collect the data for X and Y variables │
              └──────────────────────────────────┘
                              │
                              ▼
                  ┌──────────────────────┐
                  │ Create fitted line plot │
                  └──────────────────────┘
                              │
                              ▼
         ┌────────────────────────────────────────┐
         │ Evaluate significance of "r" square, and "p" values │
         └────────────────────────────────────────┘
                              │
                              ▼
                    ┌──────────────────┐
                    │ Evaluate residuals │
                    └──────────────────┘
                              │
                              ▼
       ┌──────────────────────────────────────────────┐
       │ Make a decision: Reject, or fail to reject the null hypothesis │
       └──────────────────────────────────────────────┘
```

Example:

We have the following set of data collected input vs output, and we want to calculate the correlation between them (positive / negative / or no linear correlation).

Y	X
0.70	1
0.90	2
1.03	3
1.19	4
1.35	5
1.49	6
1.65	7
1.80	8
1.97	9
2.10	10

The hypothesis test is:

Ho: There is no correlation between X and Y variables – the slope of the line equals zero

Ha: There is correlation between X and Y variables – the slope of the line doesn't equal zero

Following the path: Stat>Regression>Fitted Line Plot. The results are:

Regression Analysis: Y versus X

```
The regression equation is            This is the model of the relationship
Y = 0.5693 + 0.1543 X                  between the two analyzed variables

S = 0.0136126   R-Sq = 99.9%   R-Sq(adj) = 99.9%

Analysis of Variance

Source       DF       SS        MS         F        P
Regression    1   1.96428   1.96428   10600.35   0.000
Error         8   0.00148   0.00019
Total         9   1.96576
```

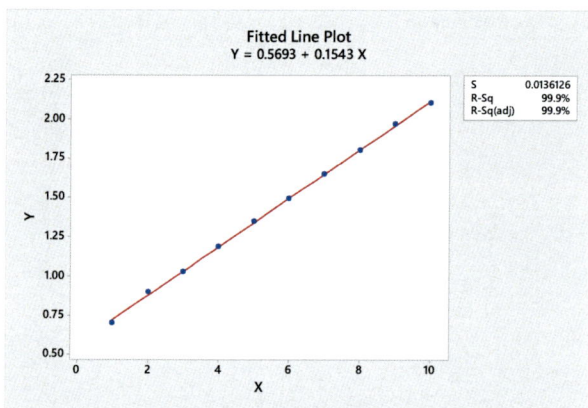

The P value being under 0.05, means that our linear model provides a good fit for the data. The R square shows that the X data accounts for 99.9% of the variation in Y.

If we need to get the correlation coefficient the path is: Stat>Basic statistics>Correlation. The result is:

Correlation: Y, X
```
Pearson correlation of Y and X = 1.000
P-Value = 0.000
```

The Pearson correlation is 1.0, which means that there is a perfect positive linear correlation between the X and Y variables. P equals zero, so we can reject the null hypothesis.

This past example was very easy, now let's move to another example with a different set of data.

Example:

For the same hypothesis test, this is the new data collected from a process, where C4 is the predictor (X or independent variable):

C4	C5
1.464	15.425
1.379	37.390
1.287	52.620
1.382	47.520
1.387	47.165
1.381	41.085
1.391	46.235
1.394	34.530
1.444	12.665
1.452	18.640
1.459	11.695
1.462	16.935
1.306	52.650
1.325	52.570
1.314	52.560
1.291	53.485

If we just follow the fitted line plot as before we would get this result:

Regression Analysis: C5 versus C4

```
The regression equation is
C5 = 368.3 - 239.6 C4

S = 6.64477   R-Sq = 84.6%   R-Sq(adj) = 83.5%

Analysis of Variance

Source        DF        SS        MS        F       P
Regression     1    3386.91   3386.91    76.71   0.000
Error         14     618.14     44.15
Total         15    4005.05
```

Fitted Line: C5 versus C4

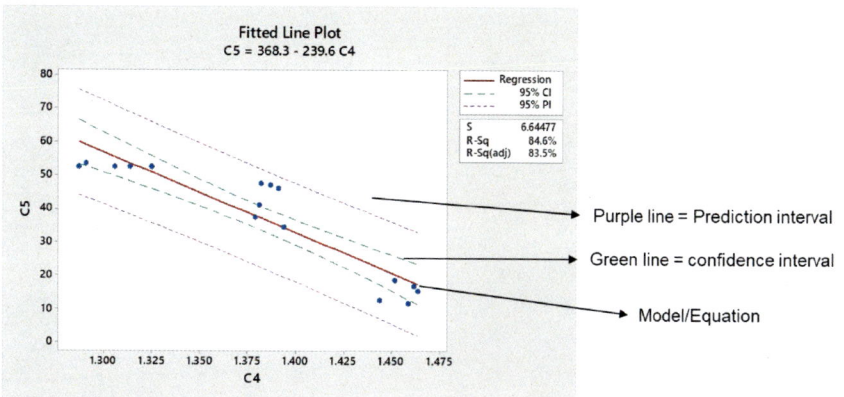

The confidence interval is calculated for the average value of the response, while the prediction interval is calculated for individual response values at the specified value of the predictor. The P value and the R square results show that there is a linear correlation between the two variables, but look what happens when we do the same analysis selecting a quadratic equation:

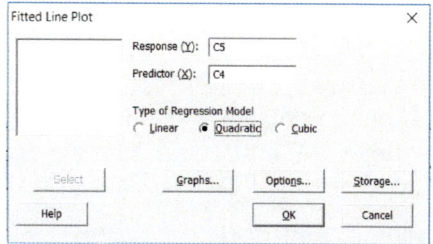

Polynomial Regression Analysis: C5 versus C4

```
The regression equation is
C5 = - 2490 + 3916 C4 - 1508 C4^2

S = 4.53834    R-Sq = 93.3%    R-Sq(adj) = 92.3%

Analysis of Variance

Source        DF       SS       MS       F       P
Regression     2   3737.29  1868.65   90.73   0.000
Error         13    267.75    20.60
Total         15   4005.05

Sequential Analysis of Variance

Source        DF       SS       F       P
Linear         1   3386.91   76.71   0.000
Quadratic      1    350.39   17.01   0.001
```

Fitted Line: C5 versus C4

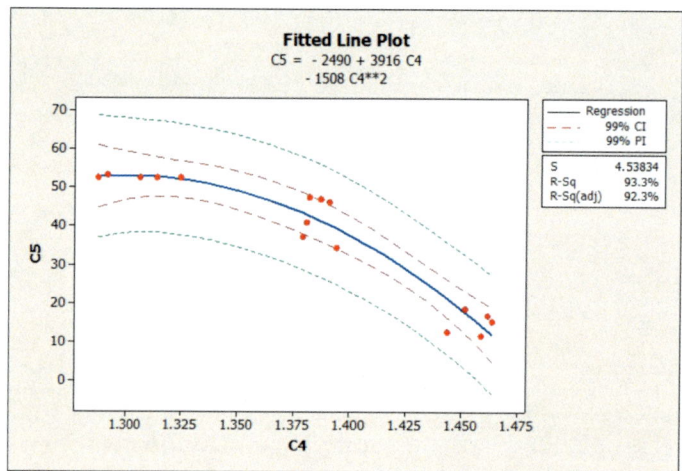

The result is now 93.3% for the r square value, which is better than the previous 84.6% for the linear model. Therefore, the quadratic model fits better than the linear model as a mathematical predictor.

The r square can be more useful than the adjusted r square (modified to include not only the collected data, but also all points as defined by the equation) as a correlation predicting model because, unlike its counterpart, it is calculated using all and only the recorded observations in the model estimation, even if they don't all fall within the fit line, and therefore is more likely to accurately predict future results. The adjusted r square is useful to compare the power of models with different predictors, specially for multiple regression (multiple predictors).

As we mentioned before in the roadmap, the residuals must be analyzed and searched for undesired patterns (clustered, non-normally distributed, out of control). For example, if we select the "Four in one" option in the dialog box "Graphs":

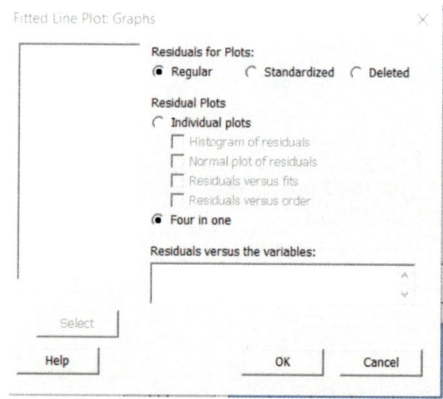

We will get the four graphs that will help us assess the residuals, MINITAB will automatically save the residuals in a different column, we will need this data to do the actual numerical analysis. This is the graphical output for the quadratic equation:

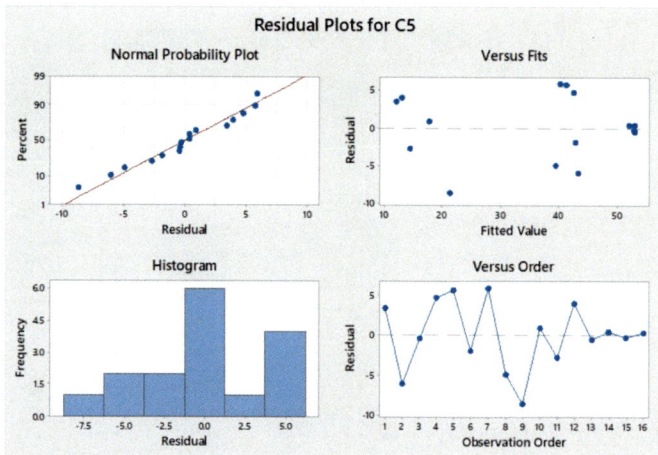

The requirements for the residuals are: they should be normally distributed, the scatter plot should not exhibit patterns, and lastly, they should be under control (no outliers). About the dot-plot, if the residuals show a straight pattern randomly distributed around the band, we can say that the model is adequate. If the residuals show a funnel pattern, it means that the variance of the errors is not constant, and the model may be inadequate. If the pattern shows a parabolic or quadratic pattern a higher order model may be required.

Analyzing the residuals from the last example:

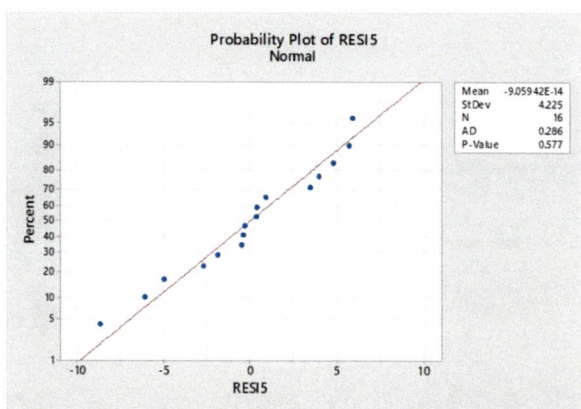
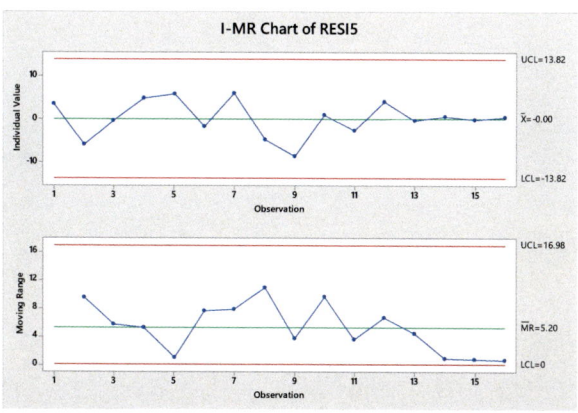

In this case, the residuals were analyzed for normality and control like we explained in previous chapters. The residuals show normality (p>0.05) and the I-MR charts shows no outliers or out of control characteristics, so we can proceed with our conclusions and make a decision based on the initial regression analysis results.

Last comment: Sometimes we expect to see a linear equation that will help us model our process, and we try to make it fit, or we settle for a low r square value when, in actuality, the best fit would be a quadratic equation. We must play with the different options to obtain the right mathematical model in order to find the best fit. If the analysis of residuals shows that there are variables affecting our process that need to be accounted for, we ought to be able to go back and re-evaluate our process, collect more data, and re-calculate our regression model.

Introduction to Multiple Regression Analysis

Multiple regression analysis is used to generate a mathematical model for a process where multiple variables influence the same process output. All data must be variable, and the amount of data must be at least 15 times the number of input variables being investigated. Therefore, if you are investigating 2 variables against one output, you need at least 30 sets of data to have a reliable study. The mathematical model looks like this:

$$Y = \beta_0 + \beta_1 X_1 + \beta_2 X_2 + \beta_3 X_3 + ...$$

This is the roadmap for multiple regression analysis:

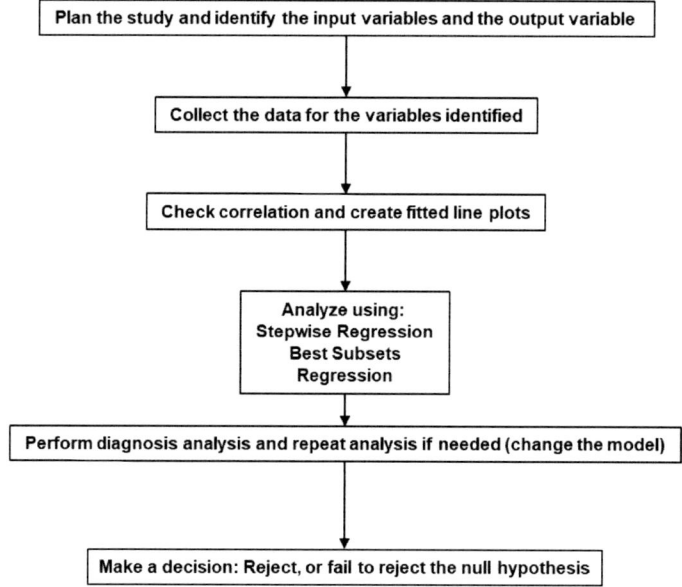

The Step-Wise method helps sift through all the available inputs to estimate the best model.

The Best Subsets method provides the best mathematical models for one, two, three or more variables once the variables are identified for significant correlations, at which point a regression analysis must be used to diagnose the validity of the model.

In this chapter we are only going to mention the Step-Wise method as an example. For more in-depth explanation and analysis, we recommend specialized books on multiple regression analysis.

Example:

We collected the output of a process (Y) and the two variables (X1 and X2) that may be influencing the process output. This is the data:

Y	X1	X2	X1*X2	X1*X1	X2*X2
1.9	274	50	13700	75076	2500
2	250	74	18500	62500	5476
4	250	74	18500	62500	5476
4	251	26	6526	63001	676
1	225	50	11250	50625	2500
7.4	224	50	11200	50176	2500
2	276	74	20424	76176	5476
7.1	250	50	12500	62500	2500
1.9	251	25	6275	63001	625
8.2	249	51	12699	62001	2601
8.1	225	76	17100	50625	5776
2.1	225	25	5625	50625	625
7	250	50	12500	62500	2500
1.9	274	23	6302	75076	529
2.3	276	52	14352	76176	2704

In addition to the first 3 columns, we must calculate the other plausible interactions among our variables in the next three columns (X1*X2, X1*X1, X2*X2).

By running the correlation analysis for all columns, we get:

Correlation: Y, X1, X2, X1*X2, X1*X1, X2*X2

```
           Y        X1       X2      X1*X2     X1*X1
X1     -0.380
        0.163

X2      0.237    -0.009
        0.395     0.974

X1*X2   0.136     0.190    0.977
        0.629     0.497    0.000

X1*X1  -0.389     0.999   -0.008    0.191
        0.152     0.000    0.976    0.494

X2*X2   0.182    -0.007    0.985    0.962    -0.006
        0.516     0.981    0.000    0.000     0.983

Cell Contents: Pearson correlation
               P-Value
```

This correlation matrix shows the estimated correlation coefficients between the terms and the model. The Step-Wise regression analysis (Stat>Regression>Regression>Fit Regression Model), shows the following:

Regression Analysis: Y versus X1, X2, X1*X2, X1*X1, X2*X2

```
Analysis of Variance

Source         DF    Adj SS   Adj MS   F-Value   P-Value
Regression      5    47.898    9.580      1.61     0.251
  X1            1     9.251    9.251      1.56     0.243
  X2            1    17.363   17.363      2.93     0.121
  X1*X2         1     9.608    9.608      1.62     0.235
  X1*X1         1     8.230    8.230      1.39     0.269
  X2*X2         1    11.674   11.674      1.97     0.194
Error           9    53.398    5.933
  Lack-of-Fit   7    51.393    7.342      7.32     0.125
  Pure Error    2     2.005    1.002
Total          14   101.296

Model Summary
```

```
       S    R-sq   R-sq(adj)   R-sq(pred)
 2.43580   47.29%    18.00%       0.00%
```

Coefficients

```
Term           Coef    SE Coef   T-Value   P-Value    VIF
Constant       -167       126     -1.33     0.215
X1            1.244     0.996      1.25     0.243   846.17
X2            0.931     0.544      1.71     0.121   247.62
X1*X2      -0.00245   0.00193     -1.27     0.235   202.73
X1*X1      -0.00235   0.00199     -1.18     0.269   846.46
X2*X2      -0.00286   0.00204     -1.40     0.194    34.99
```

Regression Equation

Y = -167 + 1.244 X1 + 0.931 X2 - 0.00245 X1*X2 - 0.00235 X1*X1 - 0.00286 X2*X2

Fits and Diagnostics for Unusual Observations

```
Obs    Y    Fit   Resid   Std Resid
  5  1.00  5.63  -4.63      -2.29  R
```

R Large residual

The P value in some cells clearly shows that there is not enough evidence to prove that there is a correlation between these factors and the output of the process, while on other cells, there is a significant correlation between these factors. The r square value shows that only 18% percent of the data can be modeled by the equation.

Residual Plots for Y

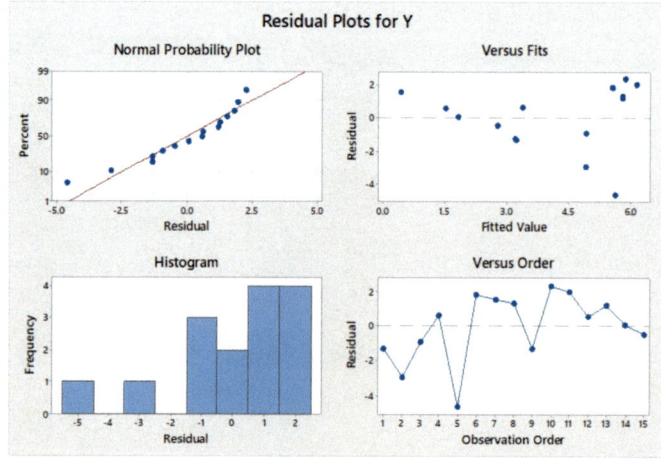

The residual plots clearly show that this equation is not the best fit and that there is a problem with the variance of errors.

References

MINITAB. Minitab© Statistical Software, is property of Minitab, LLC. www.minitab.com

John Neter, William Wasserman, Michael H. Kutner. (1985). Applied Linear Statistical Models. Second Edition Richard D. Irwin, Inc. Homewood, Illinois 60430.

Montgomery, Douglas C. (1991). Introduction to Statistical Quality Control, Second Edition. New York: John Wiley & Sons, Inc.

Douglas C. Montgomery y George C. Runger. Probabilidad y Estadistica Traduccion: Edmundo G. Urbina Medal. McGraw-Hill.

About the Author

German Candia holds a Mechanical Engineering degree from the University of the Americas, Puebla, Mexico; and a master's degree in Business Administration from the University of Texas. He started his career as a production supervisor in the textile industry and then moved to the mining industry working for Cemex. His career in manufacturing took off in 1994 as a Project Engineer in Delphi, followed by the role of Kaizen Champion for Invensys, implementing the "Lean Enterprise System" in manufacturing.

In the year 2000, he moved to Amana Refrigeration Products in Iowa as a Manufacturing Engineer, and in 2004, having been certified as a Lean Sigma Black Belt, he won the "Six Sigma Excellence Award" for United States and Latin-America for the "Best Defect Elimination in Manufacturing Award" sponsored by Minitab®, organized by IQPC (Institute of Quality and Productivity Center).

In 2007, he became the Continuous Improvement Manager for the largest factory of residential air conditioners in the world, implementing the ACE (Achieving Competitive Excellence) program from United Technologies. In 2007 he moved to the medical industry, where he currently works. After 12 years of experience in Design Quality Engineering and lately as a Design Quality Manager working on the Design Control Process, teaching Lean Sigma and Design for Reliability and Manufacturability (DRM), he felt motivated to develop a handbook that would help quality, manufacturing, and design engineers and students to solve the daily problems and questions commonly found in quality statistics in the industry.

Made in the USA
Coppell, TX
04 February 2021